CRUCIAL CONCEPTS IN KIDS' MINISTRY

Principles for Effective Ministry to Children

Randy Christensen

insigh
PUBLISHING GROUP
Tulsa, Oklaho

D1070080

CRUCIAL CONCEPTS IN KIDS' MINISTRY

Crucial Concepts In Kids' Ministry by Randy Christensen
Published by Insight Publishing Group
8801 S. Yale, Suite 410
Tulsa, OK 74137
918-493-1718

ISBN 1-930027-91-5

Library of Congress card catalog number: 2003100627

Printed in the United States of America

Table of Contents

Foreword
Preface
Introduction

Chapter One
A Eutychus Generation
15

Chapter Two
Spiritual Reception and Children
29

Chapter Three
Children's Ministry Vision
39

Chapter Four
Making Disciples
53

Chapter Five
Active Participants
71

Chapter Six
Biblical Teaching
83

Chapter Seven
Humility
91

Chapter Eight
Attention Keys
101

Chapter Nine
Your Best Prop
115

Chapter Ten
The Outward Appearance
123

Chapter Eleven
Children In Worship: Worship In Children
137

End Notes
147

Foreword
by David Boyd

Every church with children has a children's ministry. However, effective ministry to children is another matter entirely. There are many crucial concepts that can make your ministry to children successful. Without them, your ministry to children may be mediocre at best. God has clearly spoken to my heart and stated that many of the difficulties we face with the youth in our churches today is the result of not effectively discipling them as children.

As you read this book, it quickly becomes obvious that the author has a depth of knowledge and experience in children's ministries within the local church. Having served as a Christian educator and pastor for over twenty years, Randy's insights into discipling children are genuine, thought provoking, and informative. Teachers and children's pastors, as well as senior pastors, can gain a wealth of knowledge, passion, and direction as they read this book. Effective ministry to children changes their lives forever; it directs their steps by building the relationship between them and the Lord. Effective ministry to children builds a connection to God that doesn't dissipate over time, life changes, or difficulty. The "Crucial Concepts" mentioned in this book are indeed crucial for ministry designed to impact children's lives for eternity.

It was refreshing reading material written with both vision and experience in changing the next generation by touching the lives of kids today.

David Boyd
National Director
National Children's Ministries Agency/BGMC
General Council of the Assemblies of God

Preface

As I've traveled across the United States, I've seen a great abyss. This gaping hole exists in the area of a working philosophy of children's ministry. I'm talking about a lack of spiritual perception and practical application of solid biblical principles in the local church children's ministries.

I believe this abyss exists for a number of reasons. One factor may be the continual turnover of workers in children's ministry classes. It seems that adults only work for a few years in the area of children's ministry and then they move out. Some of this is easily explained. Some parents travel with their child through the nursery, and into the preschool area. Once the child moves into a grade school aged classroom, the parents become involved in grade school activities. When the child moves into the youth department, they naturally move along with their child. Their involvement is commendable. Parents should be involved in their child's spiritual upbringing.

Unfortunately, and I speak as a parent, it seems that just when I begin to understand one age's mindset, the child grows out of that stage of life! This seems to be paralleled in our churches. Just when a children's worker begins to develop the understanding, skills, abilities, and rapport to work with a certain age group, that's when the worker also moves on. As a result, a new group of children's ministry personnel continues to rise up from the pews. Most of these new folks will start at "square one." This brings a continual influx of fresh, untrained "rookies" into children's ministry who have no foundation on which to build. I'm glad they are there, but every sports coach knows that it's difficult to build a championship team out of rookies.

My goal in this book is to give solid foundation for effective ministry for years to come. Those beginning in children's ministry — the rookies — will gain tools through this book that took years for me to discover. My prayer is that the readers will gain new insight and be able to not only think about that insight, but also practically apply it! I've listed numerous exercises and application recommendations at the end of each chapter in order to aid the reader in that process.

Many of those in children's ministry today have learned how to do it through the "hunt and peck" method. They are self-trained. Or they have been taught by someone else who was self-trained. Though experience is a wonderful teacher, not all things are best learned through personal discovery. I could never have learned algebra without a teacher and a manual. So, simply, I offer this book as a manual to help those who are experienced in children's ministry also. I dare to believe that it will make a difference in their lives and in their churches. I pray so.

Many of the principles I discuss here are intended specifically for those in leadership. Most readers will be involved leading in some area of ministry, whether it be a second grade Sunday School class, a children's ministry team, or an entire church. I understand, and you need to understand, that some of the principles and applications I suggest may only be activated in ministries by those who have substantial authority. You may read concepts that you will want to implement, but you may not have the authority to implement them. If you find yourself in that situation, I offer these suggestions to you.

First of all, pray. Know that the leaders over you have the good of the Kingdom at heart. Know that they are people who desire to hear God's voice and know His direction. Pray that God will give them insight and discernment.

Secondly, be faithful with what God has entrusted to you. Apply the biblical principles in the areas of ministry God has given to you. When those in leadership see the fruits of your ministry, they will want to know what's making the difference. Even if they don't inquire, that's alright. You've been faithful, and God will have used you in a more effective way than before by applying the principles you've gleaned from this book.

Lastly, I suggest that you give your leaders a copy of this book. Maybe there are a few things in this book that would personally bless them. Maybe there are concepts that they may implement that will be of blessing to others also. I sincerely believe that. Giving them a book as a gift may show your love and support.

This book you now hold in your hands is a product of numerous influences. It took almost two years of writing and editing. But far more than that, it required years of experience previous to penning down these concepts.

I recognize that one of the major influences has been those ministry peers that God has brought into my life. There's a whole list of children's ministry personnel who have contributed to my life and ministry — at times, at late night coffee at a Fellowship of Christian Magician's Convention or standing in the dark next to an outhouse at a kid's summer camp, or any number of other events. So, first of all, I say "thank you" to those who have shared their life experiences and their godly insights with me.

The list is immense. I'm not going to try to list you all here. I realize that God has used you in His quest to bring me to "such a time as this," (Esther 4:14). I'm deeply humbled and grateful for your friendships and your investments in my life.

Secondly, I thank God that by His grace He has given me godly counsel and support through family. My father impacted thousands of needy people as an Assemblies of God minister. I am certainly one in that number. I've been truly blessed to not only call him pastor, but to call him "Dad." Walking alongside of him is a true saint of God, my father's teenage sweetheart, my mom. Their incredible influence on my life shows through whatever positive impact I now wield in ministry.

God has now entrusted to me my own family. What joy, support, and encouragement I now possess on a daily basis. It's often said, "The wife will make the ministry of the man." That's been obviously true of my oft behind-the-scenes partner, Karen. My children, Ben, Brooke, and Shane are the joy and pride of my life. I've always striven to live a life that demonstrates this truth: "The greatest children's ministry I will ever have, will be the ministry to the children who live in my own home." I thank God that, by His Holy Spirit, He often gives grace and makes up for my lack in parenting skills and grace. I'm truly a blessed man.

With all that being said, let's begin this book with a prayer:

"Dear Father God, Thank you for your unimaginable grace! Thank you for redeeming us so we may share the story of redemption. Thank you for reconciling us so that we may be

ambassadors of reconciliation. Thank you for making us not only your servants, but also your children! Help us during these days to carry your message of love and hope to this young generation. We pray according to James 1:5 for wisdom straight from You! We pray for the discernment of the Holy Spirit to be activated in our lives according to 1 Corinthians 12:7. Open our eyes to the truth of Your Word and the needs of children today. Make us into effective tools in Your hands for Your glory! Show these young ones yourself through us. Teach us. Lead us. Guide us. Change us...for Jesus' sake. Amen!

Introduction
by Jim Wideman

Randy Christensen has been a major voice in children's ministry for over twenty years. Randy never ceases to amaze me. For years, pastors who were looking for a children's minister would call me and ask the question, "If you were the senior pastor of a church who would you hire as your children's pastor?" I wouldn't even have to think about it, I'd simply say, "Randy Christensen." One of the things that has always amazed me about Randy's ministry is that he has always been a student of history but an innovator for tomorrow. Randy is always researching techniques, methods, and thoughts used in children's ministry throughout church history and then takes that study and research to create a concept and method that is fresh and on the cutting edge that is culture current. Randy has always been the kind of minister who cared for other children's ministers as well as children. Randy and I have always lived miles apart but every time I've ever gone through tough times in ministry, Randy has always been there for me, encouraging me in the Word. This book reflects these things. A study of how it's been, a look at what it should be now. It's also encouragement for the person in the trenches who wants to do what's right.

I am so glad Randy obeyed the Lord and wrote this book. It needed to be written! I agree with the tittle these children's ministry concepts are crucial. It's time we get back to the heart of the matter. Why do we do the things we do in children's ministry? Is it working? This book will address issues that face today's church and give the needed answers to turn a children's program into a true encounter with a living Christ. The measurement of success in children's ministry is not the number of kids you are reaching, or how many different methods you have mastered in children's ministry, to me the measurement is that the kids in your ministry have moved from little people who have made decisions to disciples, true worshipers of Jesus all the time, not just at church. Randy hits this smack in the head with crucial concepts that every children's minister needs to understand and know.

I have always taught that one of the best descriptions of what a children's minister does is found in 1 Peter 5:2 & 3 "Be shepherds of God's flock that is under your care, serving as overseers — not because you must, but because you are willing, as God wants you to be; not greedy for money, but eager to serve; not lording it over those entrusted to you, but being examples to the flock." We see five main duties or descriptions of a shepherd of children. First we have been called to feed the flock. Kids need the Word! But they need it in a way they can apply it to their everyday life, right now. We have been called to care for the flock. The first rule of care giving is have a relationship with flock. We have also been called to oversee. We must be leaders as well as doers. It is also important that we be willing and eager to serve. But this verse also teaches us to be an example. We should be an example of Christ Jesus. We should be an example of our Pastor. We should be an example of those in leadership above us. We should be an example of how we live and do business. We should be an example in family matters and relationships. We should be an example of how we carry ourselves and we should be an example in ministry to children. This book will equip you to become these things and more in the life of a child. I wish I could have had this book years ago. It's been long needed in the body of Christ. Thanks Randy for once again speaking what needs to be said into my life!

Jim Wideman
Children's Ministry Specialist,
Director of Christian Education and Childrens Ministries
at Church on the Move, Tulsa, OK

Chapter One

A Eutychus Generation

"...in a window sat a certain young man named Eutychus, who was sinking into a deep sleep. He was overcome by sleep; and as Paul continued speaking, he fell down from the third story and was taken up dead. But Paul went down, fell on him, and embracing him said, "Do not trouble yourselves, for 'his life is in him.' ...and they brought the young man in alive, and they were not a little comforted."

Acts 20:9,10,12 NKJV

We may learn much about children in the church today as we look at this account of Eutychus. Eutychus had a desire to hear the things of God. We infer that he had a personal relationship with Jesus Christ and desired more of God's presence in his life. He wanted to grow in the grace and the knowledge of the Lord Jesus Christ. He went to church services. He wanted to hear the Word of God preached. He probably sat in the window because the fresh air would help him stay more attentive to Paul's message.

Children today are also attentive spiritually. Spiritual sincerity and curiosity envelope our children. Saturday morning cartoons grasp their imaginations. The metaphysical is a constant part of Saturday programming. Children want to believe that a greater spiritual creative force exists. Children are searching for the reality of supernatural power in an everyday world. This is the theme of the most popular children's books, movies, and toys.

This spiritual hunger is something that is innately in each of us. Our role must be to fill kids' hearts and minds with the truth concerning our triune God, the all-powerful One! A relationship with Him will provide the spiritual satisfaction they desire. Nothing else can fill that void.

Today, children walk in awe of God's greatness. When room is allowed, true worship flows freely from young hearts as on the day of Jesus' triumphal entry. Matthew 21:15 & 16 records the children continuing on in genuine praise even after the adults were finished. Young ones do not carry the intellectual and emotional baggage that weighs adults down; the baggage that creates a barrier to entering God's presence. We will discuss this further in the chapter "Children in Worship: Worship in Children."

Many children are valiantly fighting spiritual warfare for their families. Prayers for failing marriages, sicknesses, and salvations continually rise to God's throne from the hearts of little ones. These specific testimonies come to mind.

Sheila received Christ as her personal savior at a children's crusade held by Rev. Dan Rector in Quincy, Illinois. This young girl began to ride the church bus on

Sunday mornings. Soon, she had persuaded her brother and sister to come on the bus with her. These siblings also accepted Christ as savior. The children prayed together, trusting God to save their parents. After two or three years of prayers and invitations, Sheila's parents came to church to watch their children in a holiday program. That day, both mother and father came to the altar to commit their lives to Christ. This family continues, to this day, to serve as lay leaders in the church.

Jason and Katie regularly attended our children's service. At first it was a struggle for them to come. Weekends were reserved by their father to go fishing, boating, and vacationing. Church was not the first priority. Understandably so, since their father was raised in a church tradition which did not stress knowing Jesus Christ as a personal Savior. Jason and Katie proceeded to pray. During the week, Jason and Katie would excitedly count the days until children's church. "Only three days until church, Dad!" Their father would argue, "No, we're going to the lake this weekend." But, he would inevitably find himself at church. The Holy Spirit gripped his heart. Soon, he and his entire family were joyfully serving the Lord in various church ministries. Spirit-inspired vibrancy entered their home and their lives. Jason and Katie no longer had to petition the Lord for their family. God had answered.

These children had tasted of God's goodness and desired to be in fellowship with, and under the direction of, godly people just as Eutychus did.

Eutychus probably exemplifies church young ones in another way. Simply stated, Eutychus fell asleep. His attention was not focused and kept. His flesh over-rode his spiritual desire at the time.

Our society encourages our children to be self-serving, undisciplined and spoiled. The majority are continually pandered and catered to. Self-discipline gives way to short-cuts to sensory pleasures. Children are heard screaming if they don't get a burger and fries as they walk through the mall. Three-year-olds are now offered decision-making power that formerly was reserved for teenagers.

This generation has been raised by the electronic babysitter—the television. Children's attention spans last the length of a Sesame Street segment. In general, a child's attention span can only be maintained one minute for each year he has spent on this earth. That means that a six year old will pay attention to something for six minutes— if he is interested. Churches must recognize that this is the normal state of kids today and must adjust their teaching methods accordingly. Few churches have. Dear friend, now is the time to make those changes. Wise is the teacher who doesn't ignore this fact.

Thankfully, as ministers, we do not only deal with the natural. If we operate with the supernatural empowering and guidance of the Holy Spirit, children will be captivated! No one can ignore a true move of God! When children sense the presence of God during worship, when they lay hands on a friend and see a healing occur, when the unsaved walk the aisle in response to the Gospel, one will not have a problem maintaining children's attention! The reality of relationship with the all-powerful God is not something that a person can sleep through!

This spiritual atmosphere must be fanned into flame by church leaders and committed parents. This expectation level must be set as an everyday standard. Too often our expectation level of children doesn't match God's level of expectation.

I remember as a child when a pastor invited those with needs to come to the front for prayer. Once those with prayer requests had gathered to the altar area, the pastor invited others to come and pray with those already assembled at the front. He encouraged the church body to come and uplift the needy. He said, "Let's believe God together that He will hear and answer our prayers." I remember as a child walking to the front and placing my hand on the back of an adult to join in prayer. I believed that God wanted to hear and answer that person's prayer. That's why I was there. I also remember others in the congregation smiling, pointing, and even chuckling at me. I heard one of the older saints say, "Oh, isn't that precious?"

Looking back, I appreciate that the church leadership allowed me as a young child to unify with others in prayer. I did feel a bit awkward about it though. The responses of some of those in the congregation implied that somehow the prayers of a young saint — specifically me — weren't as valid as those of an adult.

When a child lays his hands on a sick adult, when that child prays, believing God to intervene, we must be careful to not illicit an "Oh, isn't that cute" response. This response may be innocent enough, but at the same time it shows a lack of understanding on our part. Let's not forget that God uses the foolish and simple things of this world to accomplish His purposes (1 Corinthians 1:27)!

Have we relegated the power of God flowing through a child to the category of cuteness? After a while, a child no longer wants to be looked upon as cute and he quits doing that which is labeled "cute." If that happens, we will teach that child that praying sincerely for the sick is not powerful, not directed or anointed by God, not packed with faith and expectation, not a directive of holy scripture, but merely "cute." Our boys will begin to understand that prayer is not a manly thing. It's better to stay in the pew and not respond, otherwise they may be labeled as "cute."

Is it any wonder that we are losing our children once they reach the teenage years? Statistics show that the over-whelming majority of children leave the church by age fourteen. We have shown them that spiritual response is non-effective and irrelevant to their lives today. This isn't cute. We must be careful to respect the work of God, even through the youngest saints.

It is time to reexamine our response. We must train children to pray. "Pray without ceasing" should be our battle cry. We must pray constantly and earnestly. We need to openly model a life of prayer for the young ones to follow.

Jesus taught His disciples to pray. He walked with them and helped them see that the commandments of God were relevant to their daily lives. He gave them the spirit of the law, not just the head knowledge.

Today, our churches are adept at teaching the letter of the law — the facts and rules — but generally are not introducing children to the Spirit who gave us the law. Somehow we have reached the conclusion that the more children know about God in their heads, the more spiritual they will be. The church pats itself on the back for a job well done, yet our kids eventually walk away from the rules and regulations, looking for meaning and purpose. We have churches full of sleeping Eutychus'.

Our children need to be introduced to the Spirit of the law, the Spirit of power, the Spirit of liberty, the Spirit that testifies of Christ and assures us that now we are the children of God. The letter by itself can kill a kid, but the Spirit gives life (see 2 Corinthians 3:6).

This same Holy Spirit that was poured out in Acts upon entire households, including children, is still for children today. Peter knew it! He stated, "This promise is for you and your children..." (Acts 2:39 NIV). The prophet Joel knew it! He prophesied that God's Spirit would be poured out upon all flesh (see Joel 2:28). This includes the young saints.

The church of Jesus Christ must embrace the fact that children are essential members of the body of Christ. 1 Corinthians 12:14 (NKJV) teaches, "...the body is not one member, but many." It continues on:

> The body is a unit, though it is made up of many parts and though all its parts are many, they form one body. So it is with Christ. For we were all baptized by one Spirit into one body—whether Jews or Greeks, slave or free—and we were all given the one Spirit to drink.
>
> Now the body is not made up of one part but of many. If the foot should say, "Because I am not a hand, I do not belong to the body," it would not for that reason cease to be part of the body. And if the ear

should say, "Because I am not an eye, I do not belong to the body," it would not for that reason cease to be part of the body. If the whole body were an eye, where would the sense of hearing be? If the whole body were an ear, where would the sense of smell be? But, in fact, God has arranged the parts of the body, every one of them, just as he wanted them to be. If they were all one part, where would the body be? As it is, there are many parts, but one body.

The eye cannot say to the hand, "I don't need you!" and the head cannot say to the feet, "I don't need you!" On the contrary, those parts of the body that seem to be weaker are indispensable, and the parts that we think are less honorable we treat with special honor. And the parts that are unpresentable are treated with special modesty, while our presentable parts need no special treatment. But God has combined the members of the body and has given greater honor to the parts that lacked it, so that there should be no division in the body, but that its parts should have equal concern for each other. If one part suffers, every part suffers with it; if one part is honored, every part rejoices with it.

Now you are the body of Christ, and every one of you is a part of it.

1 Corinthians 12:12-26 (NIV)

Verses 18-27 clearly states that one part of the body cannot isolate itself from the rest of the body, nor should the body isolate itself from one member. "If one member suffers, all the members suffer with it" (vs. 26 NKJV).

Dear friend, one of the foundational reasons that churches are suffering today is that, deep down inside, their ministry to children is suffering. Many church bodies have grown to have a high pain threshold in the area of children's ministry. There is something vitally wrong, but leadership has grown to ignore and live with the pain. The whole local body is being affected, but they have not yet diagnosed the problem. Few look at the ministry to children in their church. We must realize that healthy ministry to children is essential to the overall health of the church.

Paul understood that. That is why he stopped his sermon and went down to embrace Eutychus. He knew that God's desire was for this youth to have a vibrant fruitful life. Paul was not satisfied leaving Eutychus in a state of sleep, or a state of death. We face the same question today. Will we be satisfied ignoring the spiritual condition of our children? Will we stop what we are doing, even if it's ministry to adults, to bring life back to these young ones? That's what Paul did. He knew that giving life to a child had to be placed as a high priority. We must also consider our role in life-bringing.

Children are waking up spiritually around the world where men and women of God are ministering to them. As boys and girls are led, they are finding spiritual life. Summer camp altars are filled with children responding to the Gospel. Thousands are filled with the Holy Spirit each year. Revival is sweeping into children's lives as churches are opening their hearts to God's potential for their children. Worship is real. Sickness is cured. The Holy Spirit manifests Himself. All of this in the lives of children!

For each individual church to thrive and prosper, the children's ministry must be healthy and strong. Any church that is satisfied with simply providing child care and entertainment for children during services—that is simply satisfied leaving the children as the "uncomely parts" of the body to be hidden away, will never flourish to its potential. The Church must believe that these young saints do not need to wait until they are adults before they may be used by God. It must hold fast to the truth that God desires to powerfully impact children's lives now through prayer, worship, and the preaching of the Word.

If the vision and commitment to raise spiritually-fit children is lacking, the local church will soon find that their children will not hunger and thirst after the things of God. Those who have fasted for an extended period of time know that after a few days of fasting, the hunger leaves, and does not return until the physical body is at the point of totally breaking down. I'm afraid that the church often looks in the mirror and sees itself as healthy in the area of children's ministry, but in actuality it's anorexic. It believes that it is strong, well-fed, muscled and fattened, but the truth is that it's wasting away due to lack of nutrition. It looks in the mirror and sees itself as healthy, but death may have already set in.

A church body possessing a spiritually emaciated appendage of children will suffer throughout it's entire body. In a brief time, the church will not be able to locate teens in their meetings either. At that point, the church may conclude that those missing teens were "trained up" to understand that Christianity was not relevant to them, and consequently their desire to be a part of the church waned. By age fourteen, these young ones found that this "church stuff" is not for them. Their decision to leave the church was not a momentary one, but one that was determined throughout the preceding years when they did not sense relevancy.

Lastly, if the Church's desire and commitment to raise spiritually healthy children does not increase, the Church will never excel to be what God intends it to be—for each part of the body affects the whole. We will miss God's will and His greatest blessings if we neglect the children.

In Matthew 18:1-10, Jesus talks for an extended period of time about ministry to children. He concludes this section speaking of a shepherd who tends a flock. The shepherd notices that one sheep is missing. He could have simply said, "That poor sheep. He really should have stayed with the rest of us. I guess he couldn't keep up with the pace. Oh well, that's too bad. But, we have many adult sheep who seem to be well-fed, so one missing lamb really isn't a problem." No! The shepherd did not rationalize why he didn't need to go after the lost lamb. Instead, he quickly leaves all and searches until he finds the lost one. Verses 13 & 14 (NIV) conclude this parable with Jesus sharing, "...he is happier about that one sheep than about the ninety-nine that did not wander off. In the same way your Father in heaven is not willing that any of these little ones should be lost." Jesus, our Great Shepherd, desires for the little ones to be a part of His fold!

In the same way, Paul did not have a nonchalant attitude about Eutychus. He did not say, "Well, that's what he deserved," or "He's only a child." Paul immediately stopped preaching. He ceased his ministry to the others to go save the one child.

These truths should compel us to go and do the same. May we carry Jesus' heart to the children of our day. He's never too busy for them (Matthew 19:13-15). We shouldn't be either.

CRUCIAL CONCEPTS IN KIDS' MINISTRY

MINISTRY APPLICATIONS:

#1. Video or audio tape one of your teaching sessions. Time each segment that you present. Realizing that a child generally only has one minute of attention span per year of age, how do you need to tailor the time you normally spend on each segment?

_____

_____

_____

_____

_____

#2. 1 Corinthians 12 (NIV) states that "if one member suffers, all the members suffer with it." To have a spiritually healthy church body, each part needs to be nourished and exercised. Let's consider your perspective on the health of your church.

On the scale below, compare the spiritual health of your children's ministry with the spiritual health of your adult ministries. (A score of "5" is the best, "1" is poor.)

Worship/Music Expression

(Adults)	1	2	3	4	5
(Children)	1	2	3	4	5

Relevant Teaching Methods

(Adults)	1	2	3	4	5
(Children)	1	2	3	4	5

Application of Biblical Concepts to Daily Life Situations

(Adults)	1	2	3	4	5
(Children)	1	2	3	4	5

Commitment to Prayer

(Adults)	1	2	3	4	5
(Children)	1	2	3	4	5

Attitude and Expression of Servanthood

(Adults)	1	2	3	4	5
(Children)	1	2	3	4	5

Commitment to and Implementation of Outreach Strategies

(Adults)	1	2	3	4	5
(Children)	1	2	3	4	5

In order to improve the health of your children's ministry, what areas will you need to teach about and model for children's workers and the children in your church?

_____

_____

_____

_____

_____

#3. Paul stopped preaching in order to bring life back to Eutychus. Are there areas of children's ministry that you need to immediately focus upon to bring life back to them? What are you able to temporarily set to the side in order to focus on reviving these areas?

_____

_____

_____

_____

_____

#4. The parents of Eutychus exposed him to one of the greatest preachers in history—the apostle Paul. Are you exposing your children to quality spiritual input on a regular basis in your home?

_____

_____

_____

_____

_____

#5. Are the children of your church being exposed to quality ministers in a kid-relevant way? Are there times that missionaries, evangelists, and other ministry personnel may step into your children's areas to spend a few moments with your children?

_____

_____

_____

Chapter Two

Spiritual Reception
And Children

Mark 10:13-16 records that people brought their children to Jesus. I can imagine a young mother standing on the side lawn hanging laundry on the clothes line. Across the way is an older woman who mentions that Jesus, the Anointed One, the Master Teacher is up the road speaking to a crowd about the mysteries of the Kingdom. A baby coos. The young mother reaches down and picks up her young one. "Yes, Jesus is near," she whispers to her tiny one. The infant gurgles and smiles. "Let's go and see him," Momma says.

I can picture her loading up her diaper bag and preparing for the extended walk to where Jesus was teaching. She knew it would be worth the walk taking her loved one out through the hot mid-day sun. Bringing her child to be in the presence of Jesus was well worth the effort! Maybe Jesus would lay His hands on her baby and God would bless him.

It wasn't difficult finding exactly where Jesus was. Many others were going to see this man sent from God also. Fact is, others were bringing their children too! As mother and child began to weave their way through the crowd to draw closer to Jesus, they were stopped. "Excuse me. Is there something we can help you with?" a disciple inquired. "I'd just like to see if Jesus would bless my child," answers the woman. "No, no, no. Can't you see that Jesus is busy? He's teaching the adults. That's the priority of His ministry you know. Maybe you can come back at another time."

Jesus saw what was happening. He saw the children being turned away and He immediately became very unpleased. Fact is, scripture says that He became indignant. "Indignant," is a strong word. He didn't simply think that the disciples were making a poor decision. Jesus became upset about it. Incredibly upset!

Clearly the disciples did not see children the same way that Christ did. Jesus saw great value and potential in the children. The disciples saw the children as temporarily unable to function as part of the Kingdom. Now, if they had been adults, that would have been a whole different story! Jesus realized that those children held eternal value just as they were. He strongly reprimanded His disciples. "Let the little children come to me, and do not hinder them, for the kingdom of God belongs to such as these....' And he took the children in his arms, put his hands on them and blessed them," (Mark 10:14 & 16 NIV).

Unfortunately, since we are adults we only see through our "adult lenses." We respond as the disciples did when we see children entering our worship services. We don't believe that they can truly connect with God because they aren't adults yet. We apply scripture to our adult lives—which isn't wrong—but, often we let scriptural truths about ministry to children slip by. We fail to see God's heart for them since we are wound up in our own maturing paradigm. We are focused on adult applications since we are adults! "Certainly God is most concerned about us and people just like us!" That is often our unspoken view. It's self-centered, rather than child-centered. Obviously, this needs to change.

First of all, let's consider this truth: "Man looks on the outward appearance, but God looks on the heart" (1 Samuel 16:7 NIV). That's what God said to Samuel as he looked upon the younger son of Jesse. Samuel was certain that God would anoint and use one of the older ones; someone more mature, more educated, more grown-up. But, just when a person thinks he has God's methods figured out, God uses the weak and foolish to accomplish His objectives (1 Corinthians 1:20-27). God isn't mandated to choose the strongest, nor the eldest. He may choose to anoint the youngest of the lot.

We must stop looking at the outward appearance and realize that God does not choose anyone because of his or her maturity. Jesus destroyed that myth when He stated, "To enter the kingdom of God you must become as a child" (Mark 10:15 NIV).

Stop and consider that statement. He didn't say that we must become as adults. He did not say that we must become more physically and intellectually mature. We must become as children.

Colossians 3:11 (NIV) states, "Here there is no Greek or Jew, circumcised or uncircumcised, Barbarian, Scynthian, slave or free, but Christ is all, and is in all."

2 Corinthians 5:16 (NIV) dictates, "So from now on we regard no one from a worldly point of view."

What is a worldly point of view? The answer is, "Looking on the outward appearance instead of the heart."

The church must learn to see children with God's eternal view instead of seeing them as immature pre-adults who must wait to make a difference as part of the kingdom. Children are now eternal souls. They are not distractions to be removed from the sanctuary, nor "caterpillar saints", who must go through a metamorphosis in the church basement before they are citizens of God's kingdom. We must love and care for them as equals in the body of Christ. The ground is level at the foot of the cross. A child spiritually stands on equal footing with an adult.

D.L. Moody was one of the great evangelists in American history. Over a million recorded conversions are listed in his biography. After returning from an evening of witnessing, a friend asked him about that evening's occurrences. D.L. Moody replied, "Praise God. There were three and a half conversions tonight." "Three and a half?" his friend inquired. "You must mean three adults and one child," his friend concluded. Mr. Moody replied, "No. Three children and one adult; For the one adult only has half his life left to give, but the children have their whole lives ahead of them."

D.L. Moody understood that reaching children with the gospel was as important a priority as reaching adults.

Moody understood the significance of each soul, no matter what age the outer body may be.

Secondly, Matthew 11:25 (NIV) records, "Jesus said, 'I praise You, Father, Lord of heaven and earth, because You have hidden these things from the wise and learned, and revealed them to little children.'"

I'll never forget a question brought to me while I was still in college. I was working as a part time children's pastor at a church in the Minneapolis area while I was completing my schooling. A mother came to me after a service and told me that her three year old daughter had a question that she didn't quite know how to answer. The mom informed me that she had only been a Christian for a short time, so she didn't quite know what to say in response to her preschooler. I smiled confidently. I thought this would be an easy one. The three-year-old approached me and her mother encouraged her to ask her preschool question. I knelt down smiling my all-knowing, educated grin. She proceeded: "Pastor Randy, I don't understand. If Jesus was God. And Jesus died on the cross. Does that mean that God died?" My naive smile vanished. I stammered for a bit, and finally shook my head and said, "Well, kind of....you see there are just some things that we really don't understand about God." I came to realize that children perceive more in the spiritual than we think they do.

To perceive spiritual things, one is not mandated to be "wise and learned." Fact is, often times one's own wisdom gets in the way of childlike faith.

Who is most likely to have childlike faith? The answer is, "Probably a child." Jesus said in Matthew 18:3 (NIV), "To

enter the kingdom of God, you must become as a child."
If this is true—and it is—then Jesus is encouraging adults
to become more like children so that they may enter into
His kingdom. We usually fight to have it the other way
around. We mandate that children act like little adults.
We want them to become more like us, but Jesus is saying
that we probably need to be more like them in some
ways.

According to Christ's statement here, isn't it fair to say that
children are somehow closer to the kingdom of God than
adults? God somehow is able to reveal Himself easier to the
simple, small child than He is to the baggaged adult. "To
enter the kingdom of God you must become as a child."

Now, I'm not saying that we shouldn't grow in "wisdom
and stature and favor with God and men" (Luke 2:52 NIV).
We are encouraged to study to show ourselves approved
unto God (2 Timothy 2:15 KJV). Mark 12:30 states each
should love the Lord with all of his heart, soul, mind, and
strength. Our minds are to be involved in our worship of
Him. God's plan is for growth in understanding.

But, somehow we've lost sight of the fact that children are
called and innately equipped to worship the Almighty!
Psalm 8:2 (NIV) states, "From the lips of children and
infants, You have ordained praise because of Your enemies, to silence the foe and the avenger." The
International Children's Bible says it like this: "You have
taught children and babies to sing praises to You." From
the youngest, God calls forth praise. Before we can even
understand our common language coming from the
mouths of our youngest, these children are involved in
worshiping God. Out of the mouths of babes and new-
borns God ordains praise. Something truly spiritually

awesome is happening. This will be further discussed in the chapter on worship.

Realize that an intellectual perceiving is not the same as an spiritual receiving. I don't intellectually understand all that Christ went through on the cross for me, yet I may still spiritually receive His regeneration! My mind doesn't perceive how His sacrifice thousands of years ago still atones for our sins today. Yet, I still believe and receive despite my intellectual weakness.

On a cold winter morning I walk into my bathroom at home. Looking through the window, I see icicles hanging from the roof. I quietly find my toothbrush and squeeze a bit of toothpaste from the tube and reach for the faucet. I turn the handle and clean cold water begins to pour into the sink. It's amazing! Where does it come from? How does it travel up through my house into that second floor restroom? Everything's frozen outside and yet the water coming from the faucet isn't. How does that work? Why does it work every time? I turn the handle to the side and now hot water fills the basin. I don't understand the process. But, I'm thankful that even though I don't intellectually understand it, I still receive it! This is true in numerous areas of our physical lives and our spiritual lives.

In John 4:24 (NKJV) Jesus declared, "Those who worship Him must worship in spirit and truth." Even the youngest child is an eternal spirit. With that spirit, he communes with God in worship. As the child matures, he grows in understanding. Truth is recognized and added.

Often, the treasures and truths of the kingdom are hidden from the wise and learned and revealed to the little ones

(Matthew 11:25). We must not fall into the trap of carnal thinking that states that being of mature mind makes one more mature spiritually. What is often counted as wise with man is foolishness with God (See 1 Corinthians 1:20-31.). At times children, in their foolishness, may perceive the wisdom of God more rightly than adults!

Charles Haddon Spurgeon, the "Prince of Preachers," states,

"I do hold that there is no doctrine of the Word of God which a child, if he be capable of salvation, is not capable of receiving."

and

"If there be any doctrine too difficult for a child, it is rather the fault of the teacher's conception of it than of the child's power to receive it."

With this scriptural understanding as a base, we should move confidently to bring children fully into a heartfelt relationship with the Father. They can receive, if we will only believe and act upon that belief. We can know that God's desire is to reveal Himself, even to the youngest in our midst.

MINISTRY APPLICATION:

#1. How will these truths affect your children's involvement in water baptism?

_____

_____

_____

_____

#2. How will these truths affect your children's involvement in communion?

_____

_____

_____

_____

#3. How will these truths affect your children's involvement in prayer?

_____

_____

_____

_____

#4. When a child asks a question that's spiritual in nature don't treat it lightly! Pray and discern how you may clearly bring understanding of God's truth to that young saint.

MINISTRY APPLICATIONS

#5. Realizing that God calls forth praise from even the very youngest, look for opportunities to spontaneously praise the Lord with a song or a statement along with your youngster, not only inside the church walls, but also during the normal daily routine.

Chapter Three

Children's Ministry Vision

Vision is basically seeing something as God sees it. In this case, it's seeing children as God views children. God knows the beginning and the end. He saw that child while he was being formed in the womb. Every day of his life is part of a plan that's already put in process.

King David shares,

> "For you created my inmost being; you knit me together in my mother's womb. I praise you because I am fearfully and wonderfully made; your works are wonderful, I know that full well. My frame was not hidden from you when I was made in the secret place. When I was woven together in the depths of the earth, your eyes saw my unformed body. All the days ordained for me were written in your book before one of them came to be."
>
> Psalm 13:13-16, NIV

God has a wonderful view of each child that we must pray about and strive to grasp. Vision is being able to see the final product even while it is in the developmental stage. Vision is recognizing potential today for what great conclusion it may be in the future.

Vision is seeing my stubborn three-year-old today as a non-wavering Christian politician in the future. Vision is recognizing the shy second-grader as the world's best adult sound technician. He probably won't be on stage, but he will be crucial in that unseen ministry. Vision is recognizing the energetic, boisterous, interrupting fifth-grader as a street outreach minister, demanding attention then as he is now!

Vision sees beyond the immediate and into the future. Vision sees beyond the natural and into the supernatural possibilities. Vision sees the final product through God's lens.

Vision determines everything a person does. If a leader does not have a vision for ministry, then he will demonstrate by default that God has no expectations for students' future successes. The visionary leader has a long-term purpose and goal in mind for his disciples. Like a long distance runner, he sees the desired finish line, even from the starting line.

Vision may deal with children's understanding of concepts, assimilation of convictions, and development of attitudes. Vision may require an equipping of children with tools that they may use in active ministry.

In many churches, very little is spiritually accomplished in their programming. Children sing songs, play games, and listen to stories. Workers get through a lesson plan, but that's all that's accomplished. I propose that more may be done. I propose that God desires that more be done!

Here is a listing of specific goals that I have for my children's worship service. My vision, and I believe God's vision, is to see these things accomplished in this ministry I oversee:

1. For children to experience the joy of worship in a large group setting.

2. To provide an atmosphere in which the presence of the Holy Spirit is evidenced.

3. To see all children become active in ministry to the Body of Christ by developing and using the gifts and talents the Lord has given to them.

4. For children to be active in prayer.

5. For all children to receive the baptism in the Holy Spirit.

6. To carry the vision of the senior pastor to the children.

7. To prepare children for future worship experiences. This includes modeling aspects of the youth services and adult services during the children's worship experience.

8. To instill a balanced view of God's righteousness, holiness, and mercy.

9. To prepare children to stand against negative peer pressure and worldliness.

10. For children to be missions-minded in all facets. This includes local and worldwide. This includes being financially, prayerfully, and actively committed.

11. For children to understand that Christianity is a daily personal relationship with Christ. It's not just a "Sunday event."

12. To make church so enjoyable that children "can't wait" to come back. If we make the church experience something in which children want to participate, then they will continue to attend, and we will be able to have a long-term influence on their lives.

Vision determines the direction of a ministry. Vision needs to be defined clearly. Vision is the engine of your ministry vehicle. It won't go very far very quickly if it's a tiny vision.

In a home, each parent naturally carries expectations for his child. Mom and Dad cheer as their toddler wobbles across the room into their outstretched arms for the first time. They chuckle with other parents about their preschoolers inept use of words and phrases. They watch their child grow emotionally, physically, socially, and intellectually. That should be a normal thing.

Each parent expects their young one to grow in all of these areas. But, what about spiritually? Why do we expect children to grow in every area of their lives—emotionally, physically, socially, and intellectually—but not spiritually? If a child is not growing emotionally, physically, socially or intellectually, specialists are called in to evaluate the problem area. Parents panic if their child is not exhibiting forward progression in physical or intellectual development of skills, yet the same parents relay absolutely no concern for a child who is spiritually stunted. Somehow, many churches and parents reserve the concepts of spiritual depth and service to those who are more physically mature. Why is this? Simply, we lack God's view of children's potential in the spiritual arena.

Thankfully, a grandmother named Lois, and a mother named Eunice were not satisfied simply with physical and intellectual growth in their youngster. They determined that they would instill the Word of God into their child's life. They knew that God had a great plan, but the child would need to be full of God's Word if he were to live out the potential that God had for him. So, little Timmy learned the Holy Scriptures even as a preschooler. Fact is, in 2 Timothy 3:15-17 (NIV), Paul says to Timothy,

> "...from infancy you have known the Holy Scriptures, which are able to make you wise for salvation through faith in Christ Jesus. All Scripture is God-breathed and is useful for teaching, rebuking, correcting, and training in righteousness, so that the man of God may be thoroughly equipped for every good work."

You see, every child needs to be taught the Word of God so that he may be made "wise for salvation." It is through the hearing of the Word that the youngest will grow in "faith in Christ Jesus." To grow as God would want a child to grow, the youngster needs the God-breathed Holy Scripture to teach him, rebuke him, correct him and train him. If a parent will impart God's Word into a child's life at an early age, that child will be "thoroughly equipped for every good work," just as Timothy was. His mother and grandmother understood that, so they started with him while he was very young.

Clearly, in Scripture, we see a direct correlation between the spiritual guidance of parents and the spiritual state of their children. Consider Isaac, Jacob, Moses, Samuel, and John the Baptist. Each of these men of God began as a child, a child whose parents had great vision for his life.

Those parents did not dictate their children's lives, but they did dedicate them! That dedication was not just a once-in-a-lifetime ceremony. It was a daily mindset that infiltrated their families' lives. It was a godly commitment that was modeled and lived out before their youngsters. These children caught a vision of what God would do through them as a direct result of the parents' vision for the children's grand potential in God.

As parents, we do not realize the magnitude of God's purposes and plans for our children, in the future nor the present. We forget that God may do "above all that we ask or think" (Ephesians 3:20 NKJV). God does not place natural age-based qualifications upon supernatural usage. Consider Samuel prophesying to Eli (1 Samuel 8:11-19), Josiah leading the kingdom (2 Kings 22:1), David leading the Israelites to victory as a youth (1 Samuel 17), Naaman's wife's servant girl (2 Kings 5), and a boy with five loaves and two fish (John 6). Each had a crucial ministry at a young age.

Children are followers. If the spiritual leaders of the children only have a small vision of what God desires to accomplish in and through children's lives, the children will only grasp onto a small vision for their own personal lives. If the leaders believe God for great things, the children will also believe God for great things.

If the children's service leader does not believe that children are capable of entering into vibrant worship, then children will never enter into vibrant worship. If the leader believes that children may hear the voice of God as Samuel did, then that opens the door for children to begin to hear the voice of God's Spirit speaking directly to them. Children play "follow the leader." They also live it.

As an eight-year-old boy, I remember going to the altar after a Sunday evening service to ask the pastor (my father) "What can I do? I want to be used by God." The Word of God had been preached and the Holy Spirit had gripped my heart. My Father hesitated for a moment and simply quietly asked, "What?" I repeated my heart's desire. "I want to be used by God." My Father broke into tears. He prayed with me, and then stood before those still at the altar and admonished them to offer themselves fully to God, even as the child before him had. The dear saints cried out to God with full hearts, inspired and challenged by what God was doing in a young boy's heart.

Friends, pray diligently to understand God's vision for the children to whom you minister. What is God's desire for these children's lives? It may be different than what your curriculum currently states. What is God's view of these children at the present, and how would He desire to see them develop for the future? Vision is always forward looking.

Consequently, vision determines instruction. As a leader, you will want to provide learning experiences that will move children toward an understanding and fulfillment of the vision. Teach from the Word of God about God's vision for their lives. Ask "What does God want these children to know? How does He want them to respond to the truth of His Word in these areas?"

Train workers to help carry the vision. I always keep in mind, "Vision is more caught than taught." You may try to teach it, but more than anything, you need to share the passion. Communicate zeal. Remember, vision is obtained through osmosis. Pray that God will help you be a person people want to rub up against so that the vision will be transferred. This applies to other children's workers and also to the children you are leading.

John Maxwell states, "The focus of the vision must be on the leader—like leader, like people. Followers find the leader and then the vision. Leaders find the vision and then the people" (from "Developing the Leader Within You," pg. 144).

"Where there is no vision, people perish..." (Proverbs 29:18 KJV). Children are dying because leaders are not setting forth a vibrant vision for what God desires to do in children's lives, not just in the future, but TODAY. We are not promised tomorrow, so we must consider what God desires to do in their lives today!

I invite you to pray this with me: *"Lord, please help me to dream bigger than ever before for the good of the children you've entrusted to my care and for the good of the Kingdom I pray. May the vision for greatness in their lives be birthed through me! Amen."*

MINISTRY APPLICATION:

Vision sets the direction of a ministry. Without a clear vision, the leaders and their followers will wander aimlessly, never truly making progress in their walk with Christ. Consequently, it's important to clearly understand and communicate the vision.

Using a paper and pencil, take time to list, evaluate, ponder, pray over, and reevaluate these questions over the course of a couple of weeks.

#1. What are the needs of the children in your ministry? How is this list affected by their family situation? Their financial strata? Their environment? Other factors?

_____

_____

_____

_____

_____

_____

_____

_____

#2. What kind of Christian leaders would God desire for these children to become as adults? What character traits need to be built and solidified? What spiritual habits need to be developed? What attitudes need to be changed? What scriptural truths must be implanted?

MINISTRY APPLICATIONS

_____
_____
_____
_____
_____
_____
_____
_____
_____
_____
_____

#3. Habakkuk 2:2 (RSV) says, "Write the vision, and make it plain, that he who reads it may run with it." At this point, let's write down the vision for your children's ministry. Here is a process:

A. Make a list of each of your children's ministry areas.

Children's Ministry: Objective:

_____
_____
_____
_____
_____
_____
_____
_____
_____
_____
_____

B. Up above, write down numerous specific "objective phrases" next to each of these ministry areas. An example: Boys' Scouting Program—To involve boys with quality Christian men who will serve as examples.

C. If the same objective phrase occurs on numerous ministry areas, one of two things is being displayed.

(1) This objective is one of the focal points throughout your entire ministry to children. It's a "hallmark" phrase which will help define all areas of ministry under your leadership. It's a precedent that pervades all departments and programs.

(2) Your ministry areas are overlapping, and you have not clearly set objectives to define individual purposes. You may be wasting your energy and time trying to accomplish the same things under different headings. It may be best to redefine a couple of your areas of ministry so their primary focuses are not duplicating others. Usually one program is better suited to teach an objective than another. Bring focus to each program so they each have their own individual purposes. Allow them to be strong in their own unique areas.

D. Consolidate your phrases into no more than two sentences so you may define what your foundational objectives are for each ministry area. You need to be able to clearly state what you are trying to accomplish in each one.

MINISTRY APPLICATIONS

An example would be: For my Wednesday night small group "Kid's Clubs," my objective statement was "To show children, through demonstration and involvement, that Christianity applies to every area of everyday life."

This sentence tells us that every week we needed to be demonstrating something to the children. There would be a learning time that was visual. Every week, children would be involved in the learning process, not simply sitting as spectators — they would be participants. Every week, we needed to show children how the things they were learning applied to their everyday lives, and how our relationship with Christ applied to these truths, or skills.

It is crucial for leadership to be clear in their objective statements. No archer can hit a target if they don't know what it is! Write fundamental objectives here.

_____

_____

_____

_____

_____

_____

_____

_____

#4. Evaluate your vision for children, then examine your programs to see if they help facilitate that vision. Don't simply read a program's objective statements and allow that to determine your vision. That's putting the proverbial "cart before the horse."

If an existing program is weak in setting forth the vision, you have a number of options:

A. Find specific portions of the existing program that line up with objectives you have. Find ways to accent these parts of the program and de-emphasize the other program aspects. Dedicate more time to the segments that are crucial to the fulfillment of the vision.

B. If your program is one hour in length, you may want to condense the time dedicated to the program to 45 minutes. Take the first or last 15 minutes to bring focus to the specific objectives determined by the vision.

Note: Using positive examples from the current program as examples or object lessons during your 15 minute segment will bring cohesiveness to your program. You may be able to accomplish these objectives by inserting this special teaching segment once or twice a month. It may not need to be weekly.

C. Run the existing program during the school year, but run the alternative program during the summer months. You may accomplish much during that three month period of time.

D. Discuss this entire process with your senior pastor and church leadership. You may be granted the option of canceling the existing program and inserting another that is more supportive of the entire vision. Note that this "entire vision" is not simply your personal vision, but the vision of the senior pastor and church leadership. Any changes need to be totally in line with your senior pastor's vision.

#5. Since children follow leaders, examine what may be done to help strengthen those in kid's ministry leadership. In what areas do you need to grow personally so you may be a mentor for others? In which areas do those under your area of leadership need to grow? What resources would be beneficial personally and corporately?

_____

_____

_____

_____

_____

#6. If you have a child in your home, make a list of some of the personality traits your child possesses that God may use in the future. Encourage them in your child. Please note, usually traits currently perceived as negative over time may be honed to be a true character strength. Remember that every diamond first began as a lump of messy coal!

_____

_____

_____

_____

_____

Chapter Four

Making Disciples

In Matthew 28:19, 20 (NIV) Jesus commands us, "Go and make disciples of all nations, baptizing them in the name of the Father, and of the Son, and of the Holy Spirit."

Is there an age criteria set by scripture for disciples? Did Jesus say, "Go, ye therefore and make disciples of people over the age of sixteen?" No. Each person who has a personal relationship with Jesus Christ should be discipled, no matter the age. The Church needs to view its ministries to believers as opportunities for disciple-making.

Discipleship requires a number of things. First of all, the word "disciple" means "follower." We want children to learn to follow directions. We want them to follow Godly examples. We desire to see them follow the commands of God. True disciples have learned how to listen and how to follow directions. God desires for us to be disciples, and also for us to make disciples. This mandates that we learn to be good followers so we may be models for those who would follow us.

I remember as a young child going to cut wood for our wood stove with my father. I struggled to go through the snowdrifts as we proceeded through the woods. It didn't take long before I discovered that if I would walk in his steps, my journey was much easier. His etched track provided a course for me to follow.

Each of us are making a path; making imprints for others to follow, just as my father did. A disciple-maker is, first and foremost, an example. A disciple-maker is one who has chosen to lead a life that others may emulate. By God's grace, may we become the kind of people that children may follow after. May we walk with the steps that will build a clear straight path through a dark world and into the Kingdom of God.

The apostle Paul invited others to follow him as he followed Christ (1 Corinthians 11:1). In 1 Thessalonians 1:6 he states, "You became imitators of us and of the Lord," (NIV). And in 1 Corinthians 4:16 he encourages, "I urge you to imitate me," (NIV). He takes seriously his responsibility to provide a model for others to follow. In Philippians 3:17 he tells the church, "Join with others in following my example, brothers, and take note of those who live according to the pattern we gave you," (NIV).

Philippians 4:9 records this recommendation, "Whatever you have learned or received or heard from me, or seen in me—put it into practice," (NIV). One of the key elements in education is observation. Once one observes, he may strive to duplicate. This is preschool education in a nutshell. A toddler watches, then strives to imitate. We think of this as play for a preschooler, but it is more than that. When a group of preschoolers play "house," they are acting out relationship and authority roles they've observed.

They try one role one time, then try another at another time. One changes a doll's diaper while another prepares dinner. One washes the dishes while another gets ready to go to work. This is a time of learning, experimenting, understanding, and developing comfort with a task or a role. A child's play is his work. And this type of play is based on imitation.

In the adult workplace, mentoring programs and apprenticeships place the novice alongside the expert to impart attitude, skills, and techniques. This developmental process is based on imitation too.

I grew up in Wisconsin, "The Dairy State." My grandfather was a farmer in the central part of the state. He didn't learn farming techniques by going to a university. He learned by watching others. My mother, the eldest child in her family, could have ran the family farm by age 18 because she had experienced each area of farming over the years. She had been tutored by her mother and father. It was hands-on training.

This is what God wants to do through you. He desires for you to set the example that others may follow.

Children today are not looking for someone that will try to be like them. They are looking for someone they may try to be like! The world is setting up models for them. Athletes, singers, professional wrestlers, and anorexic cover girls are the stars of the day. Are these the individuals we desire to have influence our children's attitudes, values, and behavior? I say, "no."

Since children are going to imitate someone, why shouldn't it be you? Why shouldn't it be me? We must be willing to accept the challenge, opportunity, and responsibility to live lives in such a way that people will desire to follow after us as we follow after Christ.

Briefly, let's examine the flip side of imitation. We do our children a disservice if we try to imitate their styles and carnal desires. Being a middle-aged man, I'm not trying to dress in the latest rockstar fashion. Some find it hard to believe that I may have a "cutting edge" ministry, even without body piercings! I have no real issues with fads. Simply, I'm saying that I'm not going to get trapped into thinking that I need to try to look like the kids. I don't need to imitate them. I need to be the kind of man that they will want to be like! And that has far more to do with who I am, than with the latest fashion trend. Children are not looking for someone who will be like them—they are looking for someone that they may be like.

In Acts 1:8 (NIV) we receive the promise, "You will receive power when the Holy Spirit comes on you; and you will be my witnesses...." Jesus did not say, "You will do witnessing," or "You will witness to people." Witnessing is an action. Being a witness is a state-of-being. It has to do with who you are and how you live. Jesus is more concerned about our being than our doing. If we will be the people He desires us to be, then "doing" will naturally follow. God is most concerned with who we BE! That's why He sent the Holy Spirit—to give us power to be witnesses.

Through the years, I have made this a consistent prayer. *"Lord, make me into the husband that my wife needs. Lord, make me into the father that my children need. Lord, make me into the children's pastor that these children need. Make me into the leader that workers may follow. Lord, please change me and make me into the man who lives a life that will impact now, and through, the future."*

Accept the responsibility to learn and grow. Pray. Humbly be the person that others may imitate.

Secondly, discipleship involves teaching and training, but it is still more than that. Jesus did not say, "Go ye therefore and teach students." He said, "Make disciples!" Discipleship is training and molding through relationship. It is not simply sharing facts — it is sharing one's life.

Jesus is our primary example. He made disciples. How did he do this? He took twelve along with Him, and showed them how to love and serve God in their daily lives. He ate with them, slept with them, laughed with them, cried with them, prayed with them, stayed with them. They came to love Him because of the time that He spent with them. They came to see that He had the truth, not just because of what He taught, but because of who He was.

Early in my life, I was honored to have a person like this affect me.

I was a troublemaker, a rule breaker, a terror to my teachers — and I was only eight-years old. My family had recently moved to Eau Claire, Wisconsin, because my father had accepted the pastorate at the Full Gospel Tabernacle Assemblies of God church.

I had major problems with the move. As a first grader, I was a straight "A" student. After the move, my grades went from superior to below average. Every week, I spent hours in detention after school. I remember walking home in the dark on winter days. I'd walk into our kitchen and find my dinner plate resting on the table. All others were cleared. Supper had already concluded long before for the rest of the family. Detention had been two hours in length, and then a walk home through the snow placed me at the supper table all alone. I didn't care though. I was uninspired to do better.

Then Grandma Harper stepped in. She began teaching the class of third-grade boys at church. I still remember her sparkling eyes as she greeted me every Sunday. Even if she was speaking with another adult, she would stop to talk with me.

She lived in a small apartment she paid for out of her retirement funds. I remember the Sunday evening that she had my family of eight over for chocolate cake. We pressed into her small apartment for that brief time. I remember how, on the way home, my parents commented how kind it was that this widow would invite our large family into her home. Not many families did.

As one Christmas approached, Grandma Harper announced to the class, "If you will memorize the Christmas story from Matthew 2, I will give you a solid chocolate football helmet." My eyes lit up. With much encouragement from my mother, I began to press toward the mark to win the prize. We would practice each evening before I'd lie down to sleep.

I remember well that Christmas Program that Sunday morning. We were to recite our memory work for the congregation. It was a full house. About seventy people were there! The Sunday school superintendent called my name.

I went to the front and began to recite, "Now when Jesus was born in Bethlehem of Judea in the days of Herod the king...." A few verses into the passage I faltered. I paused, momentarily confused. I began the entire passage over again and this time made it through the entire narrative. I smiled proudly as the congregation applauded. Then I saw Grandma Harper. Tears glistened in her eyes as her smile lit up my heart.

The next year no one offered to lead my class. We were a small fellowship. There weren't many people who felt capable, or had the desire, to lead this group of boys. We were a handful, and some probably suspected we were secretly terrorists. No one was able or willing to step into my class—except 72-year-old Grandma Harper.

"I tire so quickly," she whispered to my dad. (They didn't think I was listening.) "But I know the boys need someone. I'll take the class and do the best I can, as long as my health allows me to."

It was evident—teaching was not merely a job for Grandma Harper. It was more about sharing her heart than it was about sharing what was in her head. This was not an assignment. It was her vision. It was not a cumbersome load for her to carry. It was a labor of love, and I knew it. She was making disciples, investing in boys' lives for the kingdom of God.

Somehow, Grandma Harper sensed we boys were called of God. "God has a plan for each of your lives," she encouraged us. She saw us as future diamonds through God's eyes, not as the unrefined lumps of coal that we were. "Maybe you'll be preachers or missionaries someday."

I knew for certain Grandma Harper was a missionary. My class was her mission field. And I, now a children's pastor, am a product of the seeds she sowed. She invested her life in my life. I don't remember a single flannelgraph story she told. I don't remember the passage of scripture from Matthew 2. I remember her, and it motivates me to also be a disciple-maker.

How may you invest your life in the lives of those around you? God calls you to make disciples. This will require that you allow people time to be with you. If you want to follow Jesus' example, you'll need to be looking for people that you may invest your life in, just like He did. He made disciples. So should you.

Making disciples requires time and consistency. Unfortunately, the church today rarely gives the time to bring relationship and consistency into a child's life. Some children do not know from one week to the next who will be in their classroom to share God's Word with them. How can relationships be built and training be accomplished there?

Deuteronomy 6:6,7 (NIV) states, "These commandments...are to be upon your hearts. Impress them on your children. Talk about them when you sit at home and when you walk along the road, when you lie down and when you get up." This scripture demonstrates consistency and relationship.

There are a number of ways that I try to invest in people's lives in consistent a fashion. Here are a few:

#1. I send a monthly mailing to every child who attends church. Included in the mailing are a number of fun activities, Bible activities, and a letter from me.

#2. Every November, near Thanksgiving, I send personal cards to every one of the children's workers, letting them know that I am thankful for their ministry.

#3. I try to be totally accessible to people before and after church services. Though I may be tired from the service activities, I smile and take time to talk with every single person, whether adult or child, who wants to speak with me. I'm often the last person to leave the church. I want the people involved in my ministry, whether parent, worker, or child, to understand that I'm approachable and care deeply about their personal lives.

#4. I send letters to the children who visited, thanking them for coming. I send notes to absentees, letting them know that I missed them. On numerous occasions, parents have found me and shared, with tears in their eyes, how special it made their child feel to know that I noticed, and that I would take the time to write to him/her.

#5. I keep a list of my current children's workers with me. Each week, I try to send out four or five postcards, thanking them for investing their lives in children.

#6. When children have days off school, I try to make a number of telephone calls to talk with them for a few moments, just to let them know that I'm thinking about them and praying for them.

#7. I regularly schedule lunch meetings following our Sunday morning service. This works well because the people are already at church, it's inexpensive, and it provides time for relationship building and instruction.

#8. I try to attend special programs, sporting events, recitals, etc., of children in the church. I cheer, applaud, and compliment them profusely.

#9. I send birthday cards to every child who attends my church.

#10. I plan for times of fellowship where children may begin to know me, and not just what I think (as I preach). I've had Sunday school classes to my house for ice cream. We've floated down a creek in inner tubes. We've built snowmen and gone snowmobiling, gone fishing, had "game days," Christmas caroled at retirement centers, gone camping, and more. I want children to see that my relationship with Christ affects who I am in everyday life, not just when I'm on the platform.

Children need to understand that Christianity applies to every area of everyday life. They need to see that "fleshed out" in my life and in your life. True discipleship is established through relationship.

Lastly, the word "disciple" comes from the root word that also means "disciplined." A true disciple commits himself to standards and principles. He chooses to live by them. He's disciplined. A true disciple enters into training so that he may achieve the goal; whether that's running a marathon, learning a new skill, or teaching a preschool class.

We need to help children learn to be disciples. That means that we will help them learn self-discipline. This is crucial. Proverbs 5:23 (NIV) speaks of man: "He will die for lack of discipline." This statement clearly shows us that an undisciplined life will lead to a person's own personal destruction.

This is why "the Lord disciplines those He loves" (Proverbs 3:12 NIV). God does not desire for any one to be destroyed. Satan is the one that comes to steal, kill, and destroy. Jesus wants us to have life to the fullest (John 10:10)! We cannot have life to the fullest unless we have disciplined lives. A lack of discipline only leads to destruction.

This means that we do no favors by allowing children to be undisciplined in our classrooms. If we allow that, we are allowing them to head down the road to destruction. We are allowing them to establish life patterns and attitudes towards authority that will lead them into destruction. We don't want that! God doesn't desire that.

Here's a key phrase to assimilate. "What you allow is what you teach." Let me share that again. "What you allow is what you teach." This means that when I allow a certain inappropriate behavior, and I leave it unchallenged, I am basically teaching that the behavior has no negative consequences and is, thus, acceptable. I am reinforcing negative behavior by default when I don't correct it.

Examples:

1. If I allow a child to stand on a chair in the classroom and don't require him to sit down, I am teaching this child that it is alright to stand on chairs.

2. If I allow a child to consistently interrupt the teaching time without correcting the child, I have shown him,

and the entire classroom, that it is alright to interrupt the teaching of God's Word.

3. If I allow children to get up and walk out to the rest-room at anytime in the church service, I have taught them that it's alright to be self-centered and distract others during the preaching of the Word.

Discipline is not a favorite word in our society. Yet, patterns are set. Those patterns will either lead to destruction, or help one avoid it. If one does not help a child learn to be disciplined, a pattern is established. It is a pattern of self-rule, and it is a pattern that will eventually lead to the child's destruction.

Remember, the Lord disciplines those He loves! Understanding we are examples of God to these children, we also need to discipline those we love. If you will love those children and build relationships with them, they will follow you. I challenge you...God challenges you...to be the kind of person that others may follow. Let's be disciples making disciples!

MINISTRY APPLICATION:

#1. Review the vision objectives which you listed previously. Since children follow their leaders, examine yourself and your leaders. Do you currently model personally before the children the objectives that you have listed? Where must you grow, and what must you change to become the mentor that God desires you to be?

_____

_____

_____

_____

_____

#2. What ways may you show personal interest in kids' lives? How may you make yourself more approachable? Look for ways to be in consistent communication with children. Formulate a plan. Begin to act upon it during this next week, even if you cannot accomplish it all at the beginning.

_____

_____

_____

_____

_____

#3. What ways may you show personal interest in workers' lives? How may you make yourself more approachable? Look for ways to consistently communicate with the workers under your direction. Formulate a plan. Begin to act upon it during this next week, even if you cannot accomplish it all right now. Consider that

God may have brought these other workers into your life so you may disciple them.

_____

_____

_____

_____

_____

#4. Since, "What you allow is what you teach," it is crucial that you examine what behavior and attitudes you are allowing to develop in the children to whom you minister. When poor behavior is not corrected, children infer that the inappropriate behavior is alright.

During the next month examine these areas:

A. Preservice: What are children being allowed to do? Would their activities be viewed as appropriate by visiting families? Are the children showing respect for each other? Are they showing respect for leadership? Are they showing respect for the facility? Are they demonstrating good stewardship by helping keep areas clean rather than making a mess of them? Are things, even at this time, being done "decently and in order" (1 Corinthians 14:40)? What alternatives could be offered to the children during this time period that would channel their energies in a positive direction?

_____

_____

_____

_____

_____

B. During the service: How are children responding during the singing and worship segment? What are they being allowed to do that hinders unity in worship? Are they showing respect for each other? Are they showing respect for leadership? Are they showing respect for God? What can you do to help them focus on your service objectives? What are your workers modeling for children during this time?

_____

_____

_____

_____

_____

C. After service: What are children being allowed to do? Are there alternatives you may offer?

_____

_____

_____

_____

#5. When you recognize that a child needs to be given direction for his/her behavior, follow these principles:

A. Look at the methods that you were using at that time of your lesson. Were you holding his attention? Realize, he may love God deeply, but maybe he was bored by the methods that were being used. What can you modify in your lesson presentation in order to help him focus better the next time?

B. Examine whether or not your expectations were clearly communicated to the children at the beginning of your session. If they were not stated clearly, it's unrealistic to expect the children to somehow know what they were supposed to and not supposed to do. Everytime you gather, clearly state your expectations at the beginning of your service.

C. Were your expectations realistic? Ephesians 6:4 (NIV) states, "Fathers, do not exasperate your children; instead, bring them up in the training and instruction of the Lord." Are you setting children up for exasperation because your rules are too stringent or unrealistic?

D. When confronting a child, address his behavior, not his personal value. Share that the behavior is inappropriate.

E. Be loving. Share, "I love you too much to allow you to continue in this poor behavior, thinking that it's alright, because it isn't."

F. Be consistent. If a rule is being enforced for one child, it must be enforced for another.

G. Be consistent. If you state that children are expected to do something (i.e., not throw crayons across the room,) and a child consistently disobeys, you must show the child that you are a person of your word. You must allow them to suffer the negative consequence. Remember, if you love them, you will discipline them.

MINISTRY APPLICATIONS

NOTE: Some leaders find it difficult to carry out disciplinary procedures because of their hyper-mercy mindsets. Realize that "soft-hearted" inconsistency will breed disrespect for you and will perpetuate an attitude in which children will not understand that they will be held responsible for their behavior. This attitude of non-responsibility for one's personal actions is totally contrary to the character of God and the principles of His Word. Throughout Scripture, it's clear that God holds individuals responsible for their negative behavior and rewards them for positive behavior. We need to be examples of that to our children.

#6. Do not allow a child to explain away his inappropriate behavior. Simply state, "I saw you do this. Now, I'm not going to argue with you. When you chose to do this (the inappropriate behavior), then you also chose the consequences of your action."

#7. Some children will begin to pout and cry in order to manipulate the emotions of those in leadership. If the leader allows the child to be released from any negative circumstances due to this manipulation, the leader has just taught the child a significant lesson; the fact that if they whine, cry, or pout, they won't have to take responsibility for prior behavior. This is a lesson that we don't want our children to learn (Remember, "What you allow is what you teach."). Do not make this an emotional battle. Deal with facts, not emotions.

#8. Communicate with parents more than you think you need to communicate. Most parents want to know how their children are doing in your classroom. Make sure that you always share positives about their children also.

#9. Be a person of prayer. Pray that God will give you discernment and wisdom as you make disciples. Pray, "Lord, make me into the children's leader I need to be for this specific child. Lord, please make me into the parent my child needs. Change me. Lead me. Give me your heart and compassion. Guide me by your Holy Spirit so I may make a positive impact on those who you've entrusted into my care. Help me to live the kind of life that others may imitate for the glory of God."

Chapter Five

Active Participants

Training is more than sharing information. Training involves hands-on involvement. Parents understand that to "potty train" a child requires more than verbal instruction. It requires interaction, supervision and coaching during the process. Training equips a person to accomplish a desired task. It's not merely head knowledge and understanding.

The hallmark verse of children's workers is Proverbs 22:6, "Train up a child in the way he should go, and when he is old he will not depart from it" (KJV). Let's look in depth at this verse.

This word "train" in the original Hebrew, refers to the palate. This is the palate where horses' bits are placed. Through the control of the palate, a horse is harnessed in, and future steps are directed. Direction is provided because of the training. Sometimes this training is not pleasant for the horse, but he must be "reigned in" so he doesn't run wildly. Training has to do with harnessing the energy while guiding and directing.

This Hebrew word picture illustrates that training means helping a child learn to respect, understand, and obey the authority over him. It is a control issue. "Who is in control?" is a valid question. This training requires a leader who is willing to command a child in the direction the child needs to go. It requires consistency and commitment to a long-term process. It requires patience, diligence, and an understanding of the child's thought process and motives. Not all horses are the same, and not all children are the same either.

"Train" also refers to the palate of newborn babes. These young babes don't know where to receive their nourishment, so the young mother must train them to nurse. She does what she can to help the infant realize from where his nourishment comes. She gives him a tasting of sweet nourishment, bringing a realization of where his hunger will be satisfied. If this training doesn't occur, the child will die.

If we "train up" children in the way they should go, that means that we will be helping implant a hunger for the things of God in their lives. We will help them desire the sweetness of God's presence in their lives. We will help them realize that the only place that hunger will be satisfied is through a relationship with Jesus Christ. If this training doesn't occur, they will never spiritually live. They will grow up weak and spiritually malnourished, stunted by the lack of nutrition.

When this training occurs, and only then, will we be assured that in the end they will not depart from it. This Biblical concept of training has to do more with having a desire for a right relationship with God than with simply hearing Bible stories. True training is concerned with implanting hearts that seek after God. Then, in the end, they will not depart from Him.

Training is not just a mere teaching of Biblical facts and memory verses. It's not simply getting through a lesson plan. Training has to do with modeling. Training is about leaders sharing their love for God, and the things of God with those following after them. Then, because of that living, breathing example, children develop a hunger and desire for more of God.

Scripture encourages us to "Be imitators of God as dearly loved children..." (Ephesians 5:1 NIV). Paul also stated, "Follow me as I follow Christ" (1 Corinthians 11:1). These are key concepts in the training process. (This is discussed more thoroughly in the chapter, "Making Disciples.")

Children are imitators. Training involves bringing another alongside yourself, demonstrating to them both how a task is to be accomplished, and with what attitude the task should be accomplished. Training requires, first of all, a trainer—someone who is willing to take the time to bring another—even a child—alongside of himself so that the trainee may imitate the trainer. This may be a parent with a child, a coach with an athlete, a Bible teacher with a student, or a puppet team director with a puppeteer.

Training children requires a firm yet affirming, loving, compassionate attitude on behalf of the trainer during the "reigning in" process. It's understanding the children to whom you minister; understanding their learning levels, attention spans, and large muscle activity needs; understanding how they learn and how they're motivated. Effective training requires insight into the needs, motives, and reasoning process's of the child. Just as each horse's demeanor is different, so is each child's.

Here's another consideration: James 1:22 (NKJV) admonishes us to "Be doers of the word, not hearers only." This is stated to all believers, adults and children. We are all to become people of action, not passive listeners. Yet, a vast majority of children's ministries are not training children to be doers of the word. The opposite of this scripture is stated week by week. "Sit down. Be quiet and listen to me." In essence, the leader is saying "Don't do anything. Watch me do it all." Leaders are essentially saying, "Be hearers. Be hearers and someday when you are old enough you might qualify to be a doer."

Throughout our churches, leaders are begging for workers to be involved in ministry efforts. A non-participatory attitude pervades our churches. It is clear that this attitude began early on in the children's ministry services. People have heard from birth, "Sit down. Be quiet. Watch me." In grade school aged ministries, the same concept has been voiced: "Sit down. Be quiet. Watch the teacher do the ministry." For teens, the leader drones on, and the pattern continues to be reinforced. Then, when church attenders reach adulthood, we ask them, "Why are you just sitting there watching? Come on, get up and do something!" Well friends, I'm afraid that we've trained them up in a certain way, and they are not departing from it! We have instilled in people the concept that ministry is only to be done by the professionals. We have trained the saints to be spectators.

This is contrary to God's plan. The concept of training mandates involvement in the learning process. Action is the key word. Look for ways to involve children. Ask,

"How may children become active participants now, rather than 'hearers only?'" Here are a few ideas to get you started:

<u>Bible stories using visuals</u>

A. Allow a child to put up the flannelgraph figures, rather than you.
B. Allow children to pantomime the Bible story while you tell it.
C. Make paper bag puppets and have half the class perform the story for the other half. Allow the children to switch, and the first puppeteers watch this time.
D. Make rod puppets by putting paper plate faces on a stick. Allow the children to act out the story.
E. Display objects mentioned in the story as it is told. Each object is in a different paper bag. Have a child remove each object from its bag to show the class at the appropriate time in the story.

<u>Helps ministry</u> We need to help children understand what it means to be involved in the "work of the ministry" (Eph. 4:12 NKJV).

A. When taking down or putting up bulletin board decorations, invite children from the class to help you.
B. When offerings are received, allow a child to act as an usher.
C. When chairs need to be set up and taken down, involve children.
D. Have children help prepare and serve snacks.
E. Using an overhead projector? Allow a child to be your technician.

F. Clean up time? Don't do it by yourself! You don't want children to think that cleaning is only the leader's responsibility. Each church member needs to take ownership.

Platform Presentations

A. Have a talent sharing service where children may share a talent they have. Talk about how God may use their talents to bring honor to Him.
B. Schedule children to share their musical talents by playing or singing a song during the Children's Church offering time.
C. Involve your more verbal children in presenting object lessons. Give them the lesson the week before the presentation so they can practice and allow them to give the four-minute illustration.

Ministry Teams

The children's ministry of your church should basically parallel the adult ministry of your church. Dick Gruber's book, *Children's Church: Turning Your Circus Into A Service*, thoroughly discusses this concept. In short, if your adult service includes worship singers, why not have children help as a worship team? If your adult ministry has an emphasis on giving to missions, consider helping your children develop a pattern of giving and a heart for missions. Evaluate your adult ministries and consider where your children's ministry may be developed to parallel them. Children need to be active participants in ministry too!

Here are a number of places you may involve children:

❑ puppet presentations

- ❏ short skits and dramas
- ❏ pantomimes
- ❏ worship back-up singers
- ❏ children's choir
- ❏ bell choir
- ❏ registration helpers
- ❏ ushers
- ❏ greeters
- ❏ clown ministry
- ❏ audio technician
- ❏ video/computer operator
- ❏ costume characters
- ❏ kid's newsletter writers
- ❏ seasonal decorators
- ❏ senior citizen visiting program
- ❏ preschool ministry helpers

Don't recruit children and place them in a ministry position without properly preparing them. Train them. Training always involves demonstration, then involvement with accompanying instruction. First of all we show them how it should be done. Then, we begin to involve them in the process while we walk alongside of them and impart understanding of techniques. We help them learn the practical aspects of accomplishing the task through this tutoring relationship.

Don't stop there though! Continue on and give them God's perspective from His Word on what this ministry is all about. Share how God's love and character is expressed through their ministry. Help them see beyond the natural, physical, concrete aspects of their actions to view ministry as God sees it. Even a cup of cool water given in the name of Jesus may be ministry (Matthew 10:42). Children need to understand that.

Help them understand that "Christ's love compels us" (2 Corinthians 5:14). The motivation for accomplishing the task is the desire to share the love of Jesus with those around us. Ministry is more than singing a song or going through the actions of a drama. Ministry is from the heart. Share God's heart and your heart with these children, and their hearts will be impacted for years to come. At the same time, they will learn to minister from a loving heart.

Children are followers. They are imitators. Kids will pick up the vision that is presented to them. So we need to sow the seed. The seeds of vision and compassion planted in their lives will bear much fruit in the years to come!

Carry the vision for ministry to children and through children. Dare to believe that God wants children to walk in the power of the Holy Spirit, accomplishing the work of the Kingdom. Relay the desire and opportunity for greatness in the things of God to them. If you will pray and allow God to birth this vision within your church, you will not be able to contain the harvest that God brings forth.

MINISTRY APPLICATION:

#1. Consider: Do you see a hunger for the things of God growing in your children's lives? Evaluate: Are Scriptural presentations being presented merely as "matters of fact," or is there a hunger and desire for the things of God being modeled by you and your children's ministers?

_____

_____

_____

_____

#2. Realize: Psalm 34:8 (NIV) says, "Taste and see that the Lord is good." What can you do to give children a "taste" that may be broadened out into full-fledged "hunger" in the future?

_____

_____

_____

_____

#3. On the left hand side below, list each of the adult ministries in your church. On the right hand side, list the ministry objectives of each of these adult ministries.

Adult Ministry: Objective:

_____

_____

_____

_____

Adult Ministry: Objective:

_____

_____

_____

_____

_____

A. Examine this list. Consider which of these ministries could be replicated in your children's ministry area.

_____

_____

_____

_____

_____

B. Select your top three possibilities and meet with the adult ministry directors of the corresponding ministries. Gather information on the adult objectives, the processes they use, the commitment level required, etc.

_____

_____

_____

_____

_____

C. Present your desire to begin a new area of ministry for children to others in leadership. If possible, find another person who is willing to work alongside of you while you begin this ministry. It is not necessary that this person be currently involved in ministry to children. You will be not only training the children, but also this other adult to work with this ministry.

_____

_____

_____

_____

_____

#4. Heartfelt relationship with God is often deepened through worship experiences. The hunger and desire for His presence grows stronger as children experience a heartfelt time of worship. Examine the time your children spend in singing and prayer. Is this done by rote, with shallow unfeeling expression? How is worship being modeled before the children? (More on this topic in the chapter, "Children in Worship: Worship in Children.")

_____

_____

_____

_____

_____

Chapter Six

Biblical Teaching

Growing up as a regular church attender, I heard thousands of flannelgraph stories by the time I was in third grade. Scripture was a central focus of my home. My mother would read Bible stories to me every evening before I went to sleep. We had a special Bible story book with beautiful color pictures. I cherished that book. I cherished that simple tender time with my mother. Through the course of the week, we would work on memorizing Scripture verses at church and at home.

Now years and years later, I ask myself, "What was the point of all that?" I certainly have not seemed to retain all that I heard in those early days. But I now understand that my parents impartation of Scriptural truth was not merely for rote memorization. The goal was to mold my life through consistent and persistent input.

Romans 10:17 (NIV) states, "Faith comes from hearing the message, and the message is heard through the word of Christ." Our faith increases as we hear God's Word. So we need to be sharing God's truths—Bible stories, Scripture verses, memorization passages—so that the children we minister to will grow in faith. They need to grow in faith if they are going to spiritually be mighty men and women of God. We do a great disservice to our children if we do not systematically feed them the Holy Scripture. We need to teach and preach the Bible.

We cannot allow preschoolers to simply feed themselves: otherwise, they will grow up on a diet of ice cream and cotton candy. We need to make sure that they receive good nourishment during these crucial developmental stages. If they are not healthily fed now, their bodies will be weak and more prone to disease in their later stages of life. This is true in their physical lives and also in their spiritual lives. They need to ingest healthy spiritual food. It will help them now, and also, in the future.

Our teaching is not to end with simply imparting factual Biblical knowledge. Most Christian education specialists quote Matthew 28:19,20 (NIV). Jesus said, "Go and make disciples of all nations, baptizing them...and teaching them...." This scripture is often used as an inspirational verse to encourage us to teach Biblical facts and Scripture passages to our young ones. Unfortunately, some "experts" leave off the rest of that scripture. Jesus fully said, "Go and make disciples of all nations, baptizing them...and TEACHING THEM TO OBEY everything I have commanded you." (author's emphasis)

We need to be teaching children what to do and then to obey it! The objective in this verse is not accomplished through simply sharing a story and some facts. We are to teach them what God expects and then how to accomplish it. We are to teach them to OBEY.

Deuteronomy 31:12,13 (NIV) states, "Assemble the people—men, women, and children, and the aliens living in your towns—so they can listen and learn to fear the Lord your God and follow carefully all the words of this law." Each follower of God needs to listen and learn and then obey. Each needs to "follow carefully" God's Word. James 1:22 (NKJV) tells us that we need to "Be doers of the word, not hearers only." Knowing what to do and understanding the facts is not enough. True teaching should manifest itself in obedience.

Matthew 28 shows us that true disciples are baptized, are teachable, and have learned to be obedient. One of our primary goals must be to "teach them to obey," not just relay information. Our teaching must ultimately prepare our listeners for lives of obedience.

Focusing for a few moments on the role and position of a teacher, a wise man said, "To learn, teach." As I have prepared to teach, God has taught much to me. As I have taught, I have learned much about myself, about people, about the Bible, and about God Himself. One of the best ways to learn is to allow oneself to be put in a position as a teacher.

In order to truly share God's Word, one must be a student of His Word. In order to effectively teach people, the teacher must be a student of their needs and thought processes. If you want to learn, teach! If you want to teach, you must continue learning.

The child Timothy grew into a godly pastor, leading the New Testament church. Yet Paul continued to encourage him to study to show himself approved unto God (2 Timothy 2:15). Timothy was a wonderful spiritual leader, yet he still needed to continue to learn and grow and listen to other spiritual authorities.

1 Corinthians 4:2 states that those who are entrusted with the knowledge of God are required to show themselves faithful. Luke 12:48 (NIV) shares, "From everyone who has been given much, much will be demanded; and from the one who has been entrusted with much, much more will be asked."

What this means is that teachers must continue to be teachable! God has entrusted to us His Word and His children. We need to show ourselves faithful to do all that we can do to train them up in the way they should go— teaching them.

An effective teacher must be willing to polish some of the often used teaching methods. He must also be willing to leave behind of some of those aged methods and try new things. In Matthew 13:52 (NIV), Jesus said "Therefore, every teacher...is like the owner of a house who brings out of his storeroom new treasures as well as old." Use the old, reliable, treasured methods, but also bring out new ones for those you are teaching! Keep the learning experience fresh. Don't allow it to become stale by presenting the same methods constantly.

In this day of ever-advancing technology, a children's instructor may feel a bit intimidated. We recognize that computers, videos, television, and other interactive methods are a regular part of children's lives in this 21st century. What is a person to do if he is not an expert in all of these new entertaining methods. Can he still teach kids in this day and age?

I say unequivocally, "Yes!" Be encouraged. The fact is, even if a teacher is not totally up to date on the latest computer programs, he may teach children effectively if he will simply use a variety of novel methods.

That inspires the question, "So what is novel to a child?" The answer is, "Simply anything that's unique or new to them." Since children have such a short life experience, there are all kinds of presentation methods and styles that may be new or unique to them. This is where a teacher may actually pull out "old treasures" from his storeroom. A teacher may use flannelgraphs, shadow puppets, games, slide shows, and other techniques developed years ago if they are presented in an enthusiastic fashion.

One evening I was reading in a quiet room in our home. One by one, my three children discovered me there. They were hoping that I'd set down my book and play a game with them. I realized that I could send them away, or I could take advantage of the brief time that we had left that evening. I suggested that we play charades.

My two youngest children weren't sure what I was talking about. Once my oldest son began they all became active participants. Unbelievably, the game lasted an hour and a half! We laughed so hard we hurt! Now, whenever an evening becomes slow, my youngest son requests that we play that simple old game—charades.

I'm not advocating ignoring new methods. We should continually be developing new skills to reach and teach children. But a children's minister need not feel incapable simply because he's not producing half hour MTV-styled music videos for his class presentations. We use the old, and we use the new.

Lastly, remember that you and I are examples to the children God has entrusted to us. If we desire young ones to be teachable, we also need to be teachable. If we expect them to learn new things, we need to continually be learning. "God is not mocked; for whatever a man sows, that he will also reap" (Galatians 6:7 NKJV). If we expect children to be open to learning, we need to first be teachable. Our own teachableness will act as a seed that will bring forth a harvest of teachableness in those we are instructing.

MINISTRY APPLICATION:

#1. Are you growing in your understanding of God's Word? When preparing to teach your lesson, read each of the Scriptural passages that the curriculum lists for the lesson that week. Don't just accept the fact that the references are listed. Read it in your Bible.

_____

_____

_____

_____

_____

#2. Brainstorm with other children's ministry workers. Have they found specific books and videos to be of aid in their personal training? Borrow or buy the suggested resource to begin to expand your teaching options.

_____

_____

_____

_____

_____

#3. Contact curriculum companies and children's ministry organizations to find children's ministry training events. Keep growing as a teacher by learning from others.

_____

_____

_____

_____

_____

#4. We are to teach children to obey. Are you clearly relating God's expectations to children or simply telling stories and teaching facts? Take it beyond the rote level. Explain to children the principles of scripture, and what those principles mandate from each one in response. Every teaching session you have needs to include the relating of Biblical principles and suggested guidelines for proper God-honoring responses.

_____

_____

_____

_____

_____

MINISTRY APPLICATIONS

Chapter Seven

Humility

In the entertainment business, there is a saying. "You must be willing to be bad before you can be good." This is humbling. No one wants to be bad at anything that is shared in public. That would be embarrassing! Wouldn't it?

My first experiences in working with children involved storytelling at four-day neighborhood Bible clubs. Each day I would tell a portion of the continued story of Hudson Taylor. It was a great story, but I was inanimate and refused to do voice changes to display the various characters. "That would be humiliating," I reasoned. The children would laugh at me. They wouldn't respect me if I made myself look like a fool. I was committed to standing still and speaking to them with basically no expression. Well, by the end of the week, I would announce that it was storytime, and the children would groan and roll their eyes. They didn't want to suffer through another Hudson Taylor episode. I didn't want to suffer through another episode either! It didn't take long before I realized that the story wasn't the problem—it was my presentation style. I knew I had to do something different. It certainly couldn't be any worse.

The next week I presented the same lesson in a different backyard. I took a deep breath and decided to do a high falsetto for the voice of Hudson Taylor's wife. Hudson Taylor was gritty voiced with an accent. What did I have to lose? The kids wouldn't listen the way I'd done it before. After the week, they'd probably never see me again anyway, I reasoned. So I swallowed my pride and began. It was uncomfortable for me at first. I had never presented quite like this before. Each day the story continued. Amazingly, the children became absorbed in the story. By the end of the week, when I announced it was storytime, they threw their hands up in the air and cheered! "Hurrah! Hudson Taylor!" I couldn't believe it! They loved it!

I had to stop and evaluate. Soon, I realized if I humbled myself in the sight of children, they would lift me up. I didn't need to act like a goofy idiot. But, at specific times, if I did something considered silly by an adult, the children would love it—and they would love me as a result of it. If I could get those kids to love me, the chances were that they would also come to love my Savior. That's the goal.

I needed to get past my ego. I needed to be willing to put on a silly hat and a red nose to act out a skit. I needed to do cartoon voice characterizations and puppets. I needed to enter this wonderfully creative world of a child, so that in time they would want to enter my world. That's what our Lord did. Jesus came to earth and entered not only the adult world, but the world of the child. If he would do that, I suppose I should do the same.

The Example of Christ

One of the keys in effective children's ministry is to learn how to handle humbling situations or comments. At times we may unintentionally be humbled by others. Other times, we need to intentionally humble ourselves before God and before children.

Philippians 2 (NIV) states, "Your attitude should be the same as that of Christ Jesus: ...He humbled Himself...." Throughout Scripture, we see Jesus' example of humility and servanthood. He continually lowered Himself, rather than "lorded" Himself. Jesus was not concerned about His popularity or High status. He wasn't trying to win a popularity contest or impress people with His sophistication. He didn't demand people's respect, but openly and lovingly knelt down beside beggars, ate with publicans and prostitutes, and ministered to the common man.

Often, children's ministry may be perceived to be a "lower" form of ministry on the scale of "credible ministry." Some consider the concept of personally ministering to children as a degradation of their abilities. "It would be not just humbling, but somewhat humiliating to be involved regularly with children," some think.

It's not as visible as many other ministries that occur in the facility. It's not a "platform ministry." It's not featured in the adult sanctuary where the children's workers' peers and friends are sitting. It's not admired or recognized by those adults who are dear to us because they never see what happens in a children's class. At times, it is implied that those in children's ministry are not skilled enough to minister to adults, and that's why they are active with the children rather than with the adults. These thoughts are Scripturally, historically, and educationally incorrect.

Charles Haddon Spurgeon stated,

"He is no fool who can talk to children; a simpleton is much mistaken if he thinks that his folly can interest boys and girls. It needs our best wits, our most industrious studies, our most earnest thoughts, our ripest powers, to teach our little ones.... The wisest man will need to exercise all his abilities if he would become a successful teacher of the young." (from "Come Ye Children" pg. 157)

Yet, children's ministers need to grasp the fact that, even if others have a wrong perspective on the value of ministry to children, they do not need to fight for recognition. It's alright to be involved in what some perceive to be a humble ministry.

Jesus had a humble ministry! He had no home. He had no full-time employment. He was unwelcomed by the religious leaders. People loved Him, then they screamed for His crucifixion. He walked the seaside. He prayed in the hills. He touched the untouchable. He loved the unlovable. He set aside ministry to adults to hold babies. Many did not understand these things. Jesus had a humble, yet eternity-impacting ministry.

We would be wise to follow His example. "Let this same mind be in you as is in Christ Jesus..." Don't strive to lift yourself up in the sight of other adults or in the sight of the children to whom you minister. James 4:10 (NKJV) states, "Humble yourself in the sight of the Lord, and He will lift you up." Jesus advises in Luke 14:8-11 that one shouldn't sit in the place of honor, because that person may soon be moved down to sit in the least important place. Be faithful, and don't worry about being invited up!

Once, I was complaining about not being recognized as I thought I should. A friend of mine said to me,

"Remember, Randy, it won't be long, and we'll be able to go first in line." For Mark 10:31 talks about how at the last day, the last will be able to go first. God is just. Recognition is in His hands. I don't need to be concerned about it, because in the end, God will do what is right.

Colossians 3:23 (NIV) encourages us to minister, "...as working for the Lord, not for men." Our focus needs to be upon doing what Jesus would have us do. We are working for recognition from Him, not from others.

Ministering To Children

It's Biblically reasonable to expect children to display good manners and respect for authority. Scripture states that all should respect and honor those who are in ministry (1 Timothy 5:17). Unfortunately, some children have not been trained to show respect to leaders. They honestly don't know how. They've never been trained. It's never been modeled to them. Television shows, secular conditioning, and poor home training have conditioned children's negative responses and non-responses to authority. Training will need to be lovingly administered.

At times, adult leaders have a difficult time humbling themselves before children. Adults want to be respected and their work to be respected. The natural response is for a leader to try to demand respect from children. An iron-fist approach is often implemented. "You will show respect to me, or else!" is voiced. Emotionalism is often the key to this approach. The leader is personally offended and is emotionally wounded because of the lack of displayed respect.

May I offer another approach to gaining children's respect? This is simply it: humble yourself. I'm not saying, "Let the children run all over you." I'm saying, "humble yourself." "Let this mind be in you that was in Christ Jesus..." (Philippians 2:5 NKJV). If you want to be a true leader, you must be the servant of all (Mark 10:43-45). It's an oxymoron. Scripture promises, if you will humble yourself, you will be lifted up (James 4:10).

Ask yourself, "What are the needs of these children?" Then ask yourself, "How may I meet the needs of these children?" It's probably different than the listed curriculum objective for the lesson of the day. If you start to meet the needs of the children God has entrusted to you, they will honor you and respect you. You won't need to demand their respect. It will naturally come. Respect does not come because of a title. Respect is earned through relationships. Respect grows because of the relevancy of the teaching you bring to your disciples' lives. Obedience may be demanded, but respect cannot be. As the old television commercial said, "...you earn it."

Earn the respect of your kids by humbling yourself and becoming part of their world. That's what God did. He left the riches and wonders of heaven, humbled Himself, and entered our world. He became like us, so in time, we may become like Him. He suffered so that we could have an example of endurance. He took on the form of man to illustrate to us what it means to be the children of God. He entered our world so that we would be able to enter His world! We, as children's leaders, need to do the same. We need to humble ourselves and enter the world of those to whom we are ministering.

What does a child's world consist of today? What are their interests? What are their fears? What areas of entertainment are kids absorbed by today? What are the styles? What music do they listen to? Who are the popular role models? What are the fads? These questions need answers if you are going to enter into the world of the children you minister to today.

Please understand that I'm not saying that you need to dress like children. You don't need to adopt all their lingo and watch their favorite television programs continuously. You should watch some of them, though! You need to be able to speak knowledgeably about the common things in their lives. Jesus humbled Himself and became part of our world, but He was still an individual — not just an imitation of the popular culture of the day. You don't need to be imitating everything children are doing today. But, you should be aware of it and use it in your teaching so that children will sense relevancy to their everyday lives.

I realize that in children's ministry we must often force ourselves to offer presentations that may not be as polished as we would like them to be. Sometimes that is humbling. We simply don't do as well as we would like to do. We have regular time deadlines for services and classes on a weekly basis and only so much time to use in preparation. It's not realistic to expect oneself to compete with Disney with only three days to prepare!

Don't allow yourself to feel downtrodden! Thank God that He understands your time schedule. He knows your priorities. Hold to the fact: "In the same way, the Spirit helps us in our weakness" (Romans 8:26 NIV). We may not be as proficient as we desire to be. If we feel that way, that's good! That means that we have motivation to improve our presentations for the glory of God. But, do not allow yourself to be disheartened.

First of all, remember that the Lord is going to help you present His word, even though your methods may be a little weak. God's Word is life-changing. It's living and active (Hebrews 4:12). It will accomplish what God is sending it out to do (Isaiah 55:11).

Secondly, know that the more you work at something, the better you'll become. The key to becoming good at something is summed up in this one word — practice.

How did Shari Lewis become an expert ventriloquist? Practice. How did Marcel Marceau become a wonderful pantomimist? Practice. How did Michael Jordan become the preeminent all-star basketball player? Practice. How will you become a wonderful storyteller? Practice. That practice time needs to be done before you get in front of an audience. We will look further into this area in the chapter, "Your Own Best Prop."

Children will appreciate your effort to connect with them. They will honor you if you are playful, not if you act like Ebenezer Scrooge. You will endear yourself to them if you will enter their world, rather than try to force them into yours. If you will humble yourself to win their hearts, you will have the opportunity to guide them to Jesus.

Humility. It's a choice that each leader has to make for himself. The Lord resists the proud, but he elevates the humble (Proverbs 3:34). Kids do too.

MINISTRY APPLICATION:

#1. Have you felt downhearted at times because you are not in a ministry visible to other adults (your peers)? Read Matthew 18:1-14 and Matthew 6:1-4. What is God saying to you through these scriptures? Remember: what you are offering "behind-the-scenes," will be honored by our Lord.

_____

_____

_____

_____

_____

#2. Do you feel embarrassed while teaching children? What method that may be effective in ministry do you avoid because you feel foolish when presenting it? (i.e., puppets, clowning, singing, etc.) Intentionally schedule yourself to present part of your lesson using this method. Practice diligently. Pray, then present. Afterwards, examine how the children responded during your presentation. You may endear yourself to your students as you humble yourself before them!

_____

_____

_____

_____

_____

Chapter Eight

Attention Keys

Sitting in a metal pole barn, one hundred and forty children dripped sweat. The temperature had lowered to eighty-seven degrees outside. Earlier in the day, the building was cooked by temperatures ten degrees hotter. No air conditioning existed. As children dripped, the Holy Spirit poured Himself into the room. As puppets sang, clowns laughed, and object lessons were viewed, the Word of God became real in hearts and lives. Incredibly, that night over forty children received the infilling of the Holy Spirit. Hearts were full and praise was vibrant! Lives were changed as God showed Himself to be real.

We are careful to give God all of the glory for the positive results in that service. Anything spiritually impacting comes only from Him. "Not by might, nor by power..." ...nor by puppets, clowns, illusions or jokes... "...but by my Spirit' saith the Lord" (Zechariah 4:6 KJV). None of these methods can change a person's life by itself.

Yet, a presentation principle exists here. Children focused because they were given a focal point. The leader used visuals that were unique and interesting. Costumed characters and puppets brought novel personalities into learning situations. Children wanted to watch and listen to these out-of-the-ordinary characters. The presentation techniques and methods motivated children to focus. They were teaching aids—aids that helped children focus on and assimilate the spiritual message.

In children's services, I've found that it's a lot easier to teach children when they want to pay attention. What that means is that I need to find what they are interested in and then use that object or method to present my message. If they are interested in cartoon characters, I use puppets and clowns. If they are interested in videos, I use videos. If they are interested in stories, I present a drama or tell a story with visuals. It's a lot easier to teach them when they want to pay attention!

When I was eleven-years old, I was kicked out of Children's Church—not for just that one Sunday, either. The Children's Church leader said, "Don't come back. You are done in here." Now, I don't blame her. But you need to understand...I loved God. I truly did. But, I was bored. In my eleven years as a pastor's son, I had watched an infinite amount of flannelgraph stories. I knew all of the songs. I was energetic, inquisitive, and fun loving. I loved God, but my attention was not being commanded by the presentation. Since I was not excited by the presentation, I decided to make my own excitement. I did, and from that time on, I sat on the wood pew next to my mother in the adult service.

Today, I have the challenge of working with eleven-year old boys. There are times when I notice their attention is not focused on what I'm doing. This requires that I first evaluate, not the spiritual maturity of the child, but my presentation methods! The responsibility rests first of all on me. "What am I doing that does not hold their interest? What can I do that they will want to give their attention to?" I must ask, "How can I make this more interesting?"

Children do need to learn self-discipline, but shouldn't our teaching about our exciting, creative, life-giving God be exciting, creative, and life-giving? Fact is, it shouldn't be the children's minister's responsibility to try to teach self-discipline to a child in only one-hour-a-week! Self-discipline needs to be first and foremost taught in the home. The children's minister's key role should not be as a disciplinarian, but as a loving minister.

I often ask myself, "If I were a child, would I want to pay attention to this presentation?" If my answer is "no," then I had better look for another way to present the message. Children are far more into the entertainment media of the day than are adults. Be aware that they are accustomed to being entertained and taught in "sound bytes." This generation has been raised with Sesame Street. "One, two, three, four, five, six, seven, eight, nine, ten....this program has been brought to you by the letter 'r.'" The attention span is short and everything is visual. This is the music video generation. The picture on the screen changes every three seconds or less.

So what is a children's ministry leader to do? First of all, use multiple methods so children will want to pay attention. You may have the same format for your class each time, but simply use different methods from week to week within that format. For example, you may have a story time each class session. Simply, use a variety of visuals in your storytelling. One week use dressed up teddy bears.

Another time use the flannelgraph. The next time act out the story with puppets or use a Bible Story video. Variety is the spice of a class session. Parents should note that the same is often true for family devotions.

Though many creative children's ministers hate the quote, "We've never done it that way before," when said by another in the church, they often personally use that exact same statement when it comes to using new presentation methods. Many find one or two ways of storytelling, or teaching a Scripture verse, or illustrating a message, and then never try any other ways. Leaders are uncomfortable presenting methods they haven't mastered, so children are required to sit through the same—styled presentations week after week. "We've never done it that way before," becomes an easy reason for a teacher to not try something new. Don't forget, variety is the spice of a lesson! Change your methods. You may be bad at them at first. But the more you practice them, the better you will become. If you will give your students a break by sharing the Word of God with a different method, then the children will actually react stronger when you go back to the method with which you are most comfortable.

Here's a listing of techniques and visuals I recommend practicing and using in ministry:

- ❑ storytelling
- ❑ juggling
- ❑ shadow screens
- ❑ mime
- ❑ home videos
- ❑ illusions

- ❑ clowning
- ❑ costume characters
- ❑ puppets
- ❑ songs
- ❑ ventriloquism
- ❑ overhead stories
- ❑ cartooning
- ❑ raps
- ❑ slide presentations
- ❑ origami
- ❑ music backgrounds
- ❑ chalk art
- ❑ character voices
- ❑ masks

When teaching a Scriptural concept, find an object you may use to illustrate the truth. As you present the object lesson, it gives the child a focal point. You will find that when you have something in your hand, people are more apt to give you their visual attention. They will look at you to see what you are going to do with the object.

Jesus used this method in His teaching. When asked if taxes should be paid, He replied, "Show me a coin." He then taught the lesson from the object He held in His hand (see Matthew 22:16-22). While sitting on the Mount, He talked about the lilies of the field (Matthew 6:28). I believe He either picked one or pointed to one as He spoke. He probably pointed to "a city set on a hill" as he spoke about it (Matthew 5:14). When a woman caught in adultery was brought before him for judgment, Jesus bent over and drew in the sand. We are not sure what He drew, but it was probably something that impacted the accuser's hearts. It was after He verbally responded and then drew on the ground that they began to go away (John 8:3-11). Jesus used visuals.

Deuteronomy 6:8,9 (NIV) says, "Tie them as symbols on your hands and bind them on your foreheads. Write them on the door frames of your houses and on your gates." In this passage, God instructs leadership to use visuals in the teaching of His commands. It's Scriptural to use focal points.

The Lord told Joshua to have Israelite men carry boulders from the bed of the Jordan River and place them in a pile on the shore. Why would he command that? It was so families would see the pile as they traveled. They would see the stones and be reminded of what God had done for the nation of Israel as they came from the wilderness into the land of Promise (Joshua 4). This rock pile became a focal point from which generations to come would teach and more easily remember the lesson. Once again, we see God promoting use of visuals as teaching aids!

To take the use of visuals one step further, ask yourself this question, "May the children touch or handle the object?" If they can without damaging it, let them. When teaching about having a "soft heart," allow children—even just one child—to form a heart out of playdough. When speaking on being blinded by sin, partners may blindfold each other and try to make it to a goal line. When instructing about giving up bad thoughts or fears or sin, have children write one of those on a piece of paper and thumb tack it to a wooden cross. Make learning interactive. Spiritual learning needs to not only be intellectually perceived, but also applied and experienced!

Some objects I've used for spiritual lessons:

OBJECT	THEME
oatmeal	Sometimes you have to force yourself to eat it. That's like Bible reading.
pickles	You can be a friend who's sour, or a friend who's sweet.
bicycle nut	Don't feel insignificant. Each little part has a specific job (or talent).
live animals	God cares for us or obedience or talk about their homes or unique attributes that prepare them for whatever they may encounter. God knew!
raw egg	Don't ignore God's laws. (Like the law of gravity.) Ignoring God's laws can mess a person up!
sports uniform	Just because you dress like an athlete doesn't mean you are one, and just because you dress like a Christian doesn't mean you are one.
spring snakes in a can	It's impossible to take back your words once you let them fly out!

OBJECT	THEME
television antenna	When you lift your arms in worship, it may help you get in tune with God.
yo-yo	When you are feeling down, think of the good things that God has done, and it will lift you back up!
dirty drinking cup	Man looks on the outward appearance, but God looks on the heart.
radio	We need to pause, focus, and tune-in to what God is saying to us.
silverware (spoon, fork, knife, etc.)	We each are much the same, yet we each have unique abilities.

Use the novel or unique. Illustrations with illusions, grandpa's false teeth, or a comedy character with a wacky personality, may be just what is needed. It doesn't have to be new technology to be unique to children. Remember, "Children are not stupid, just inexperienced." Because they don't have the life experience you've had, they also haven't seen many of the things that you've seen. Use this to your advantage. I regularly pull unique props out of my storage closet. My closet is full of stuff I've had since I was a child. When I was a child these things weren't unique, but today's children have never seen these objects before so they appear new to them!

One evening, I had a group of older-aged grade schoolers over to my house. We watched a video of Charlie Chaplin and ate popcorn. About twenty minutes into the video a girl asked, "Why isn't he talking?" I took time to explain that these were silent movies since when they were made the producers didn't have the technology to put sound with film. The children were amazed! Another ten minutes later another said, "Hey, I know that guy! He sells computers!" I had to laugh. IBM computer had been using the Charlie Chaplin image in some of their advertising. I was once again able to impart some knowledge. The truth of the matter is, often something may be old enough that it will seem new! Just consider the clothing styles of the day—enough said.

Secondly, children will pay attention if you build a relationship with them. Most children would trade every video-game in the world for the sense that someone truly, dearly loved them. One church I worked at had a wonderful Saturday bus ministry. Even on winter Saturdays, children would get out of bed, dress themselves, and trudge through the snow to the bus. They could've stayed home and watched Saturday morning cartoons. They had been in school all week. This was their "day off." But they came to church. Why? Their parents were not encouraging them to attend. Some of their parents didn't even get out of bed to see them head out the door. I don't believe it was because of our programming that children came either. It was because every person who stepped on that bus was met by loving workers.

One Saturday, one of my gentlemen who worked on the bus told me the story of how a little five-year-old girl climbed on his lap on the bus and asked if he would be her daddy. With tears in his eyes he replied, "Every Saturday morning when you get on this bus, I'll be your daddy while we are together." Nothing will ever compete with a caring heart. Children can tell if a worker is faking it, or if they are truly loved.

Lastly, children will pay attention if they sense the message is relevant to their life. It cannot be merely head knowledge. It cannot be simply a curriculum. Children need to understand that Christianity applies to every area of their everyday life. That only comes as you use relevant illustrations that they sense to be pertinent. Use illustrations and applications that relate to their lives at school, on the bus, in the neighborhood, and in their families. Explain not only what the Bible says, but how it is fleshed out in everyday life. Jesus understood that we needed the Word, but we also needed the Word fleshed out! That's why He came, so the Word would become flesh! He wanted God's message to be relevant to where we live everyday. We also need to take the Word of God and flesh it out for these children.

People sense the relevancy of the message, only after they sense the relevancy of the presentation method. If the presentation of the message is uninteresting, they will conclude that the message must not be applicable to their lives. When an adult sits on a padded pew during an unenthusiastic sermon, the adult's mind wanders from the topic of lunch, to the new hair coloring of Sister Snodgrass, to the behavior of the children seated ahead two rows on the other side of the sanctuary, to football. Most adults have learned to discipline themselves to sit and look at the speaker through this whole event, but they have not really heard the Word. The preacher may have delivered a Scriptural message full of life-changing content, but due to his presentation style, the message was not received. They were bored, so they concluded that the message was irrelevant.

On the other hand, if the presenter understands and accommodates the attention span of his audience, if he finds illustrations and visuals to which his congregation can relate, if he engages his audience through practiced skills and well-timed speech, the listeners will gladly give his presentation their full attention. That's what we want. We want our listeners to give their full attention to the biblical message we are sharing—whether they are adults or children.

In closing—pour your heart into these children. Share your life with them. Find the unique and work on having variety. Practice a variety of skills, and you will be able to hold children's attention. It requires work during the preparation stage, but it's a lot less work during the presentation stage when kid's stay focused. You'll find that it's a lot easier to teach children when you make it so they want to pay attention!

MINISTRY APPLICATIONS:

#1. Over the next six weeks, write down each method that you use in class for:

A. Telling your Bible story.
B. Teaching your Scripture memory verse.
C. Making your craft.
D. Involving children in the learning process.

_____

_____

_____

_____

_____

_____

_____

_____

Examine: Is there variety? Remember, "The only bad method, is the one you use all the time."

#2. Brainstorm with other teachers about methods they have used in teaching. Intentionally schedule yourself to try a few methods that are new to your teaching style.

_____

_____

_____

_____

_____

_____

#3. When preparing your lesson this week, look for specific objects that are mentioned in the story. Are you able to find these objects? (Maybe miniature ones.) Place them in front of the children during that portion of your message to help hold their focus.

_____

_____

_____

_____

_____

#4. How can you show your children that you truly care about them? Are you able to arrive a few minutes earlier so you may simply talk with children about the activities in their lives? What type of small gift could you give them that shows each one that he or she is special to you?

_____

_____

_____

_____

_____

MINISTRY APPLICATIONS

Chapter Nine

Your Best Prop

Years ago I trained for ministry under the direction of Rev. Dan Rector. "Big Dan," as we called him, was integral in my development as a children's pastor and evangelist. He told of a friend of his who traveled to conduct children's meetings. This friend flew into an airport on the same day on which he was to begin the services. The gentleman arrived at the airport, but, unfortunately, his luggage didn't. What was the evangelist to do? Since he did not have his props, puppets, or materials, the evangelist canceled the service for that evening.

Ever since "Big Dan" shared that story with me, I've purposed in my heart to not be totally dependent upon props and teaching aids. I must have skills that are developed that cannot be lost in baggage claim somewhere! I've determined that a children's pastor should be his own best prop.

As a child I learned to play piano. This has become an integral part of my leading children in worship. It was a talent that was already developed that I could use. As I began ministering to children, I purposed to learn puppetry and clown ministry. Both are cartoon-type characters who use comedy, exaggeration, and misunderstanding. After working at these areas diligently to reach a certain level of proficiency, I moved on to learn storytelling techniques. After that, I worked to strengthen my juggling skills and began to learn ventriloquism. After becoming somewhat proficient in those areas, I began to work on mime. One step at a time. I didn't strive to become good at all of them at the same time. I set goals for specific technique mastery over a period of years and focused on each at different times.

This process has been going on now since the fall of 1980. I'm still not as proficient in many areas as I'd like to be, but I'm on the way. Will Rogers quipped, "Even if you're on the right track, if you just sit there, you'll get run over." We need to be on the right track, but we also need to be making progress!

I worked on ventriloquism for about three years before I ever used it in public. It's been my goal to show my audiences what I can do, not what I can't do! I'm not a great ventriloquist, but I'm now at a level where my audience can enjoy it because I don't have to concentrate so hard on the technical aspects of the method.

That's the first key: learn the technique thoroughly. After that, it can become entertaining and effective. Learn the basics of a method. Practice them, then practice again. Videotape your practice times and your presentations. Review them so you may see what your audience sees. Learn what you can do better. Don't be satisfied with being poor.

I once heard that the Rev. Billy Graham said, "A sermon is not a good sermon until it has been preached twenty times." In order to establish a continuity of thought, in order to be able to present a lesson without having to stop and concentrate on the subject material, you need to go through it a number of times. Be hard on yourself here. Preparation + Practice = Quality Presentation. Poor preparation and non-existent practice never results in a quality presentation.

For some errant reason, the church has had the idea that children's work requires less skill and preparation than adult work. I've found it to be totally the opposite. In preparation to minister to adults or children, I need to thoroughly pray and be led by the Holy Spirit as I pen the message. For adults, I simply get up and speak. With children, I need to break it down into simpler vocabulary and find visuals, stories, and illustrations that will make the message clear. In order to present the Word of God with clarity to a second grade child, I need to clearly understand it. I can't use Christian church verbiage and expect a child to understand. Consequently, working with children has made me a better preacher for adults. I've been forced to have clarity, simplicity, and effective illustrations.

Psalm 33:3 (NIV) tells us to "play skillfully," as we worship our Lord. That means that we don't offer God something that's poorly done and expect that He'd be honored. 2 Corinthians 13:11 (NIV) states, "Aim for perfection." We understand that we probably won't "hit" perfection, but we should at least be aiming in that direction! Don't be satisfiedwith poor presentation. Aim high.

Don Shula coached the National Football League's only team that ever went undefeated through an entire season. Coach Shula states, "Without striving for perfection, excellence is never attained." It was obvious that his team had striven for perfection. They were excellent.

Years ago, while traveling as a children's evangelist, I stepped into a church foyer and heard two children's church leaders greet each other in the foyer. One stated, "Aren't you leading Children's Church today?" "Oh no, I thought you were!" They both laughed. Neither had planned to be with the children. The first stated, "Well, I'll go downstairs and lead a couple songs if you'll pull out a flannelgraph story to tell the kids." They both giggled together about their little slip up and somehow didn't seem to grasp the gravity of the situation. Children's souls hung in the balance. They didn't grasp that.

I read in a national denomination's Christian education publication about how their curriculum was the best because it "required no special preparation or skills on behalf of the teacher." This is a sad commentary on that denomination's approach to children's ministry. This type of statement clearly perpetuates the concept that working with children requires no serious preparation. This is contrary to educational standards and the Word of God.

Charles Haddon Spurgeon, the Prince of Preachers stated:

> Never go to your class with the thought that the children cannot comprehend you; for if you do not make them understand, it is possibly because you do not yourselves understand; if you do not teach children what you wish them to learn, it may be because you are not fit for the task; you should find out simpler words, more fitted for their capacity, and then you would discover that it was not

the fault of the child, but the fault of the teacher, if he did not learn ("Come Ye Children," p. 100).

John chapter 2 records Christ's first miracle. While at a wedding in Cana, the host ran out of wine. Mary, the mother of Jesus, told the servants to do whatever Jesus told them to do. Verse seven (NIV) relays: "Jesus said to the servants, 'Fill the jars with water'; so they filled them to the brim." The ministry principle we must grasp is this: You do all that you can do, then let Jesus take it from there. The servants didn't just fill those huge clay jars half full. They filled them to the brim! They did all they could do and then God did the miracle!

Too often, we expect the Holy Spirit to do it all! We need to do our best as we prepare and then humbly offer our best to God the Father and His children! 2 Timothy 2:15 (KJV) states, "Study to show yourself approved unto God, a workman that needs not be ashamed, rightly dividing the word of truth." We need to study. We need to be workmen, and that requires work!

In the fall of 1980 I sang in the North Central Bible College Chorale. I will never forget our first outing. We sang the wonderful old hymn, "Sun of My Soul." Unfortunately, I had not put in the time to learn the second verse well. No worry—I knew if I could hear the person next to me sing the first word or two of the second verse, it would spark my memory and I would be able to jump right in singing. No one would even notice.

As we began to sing the second verse, to my surprise and my horror I discovered that the person next to me was in the same predicament as I was. So was the person on the other side of me, and behind me, and the person on the other side of him, and on through the entire chorale. By the end of the second verse, only a half dozen out of the forty voice choir were still singing. It was terrible!

Following that service, the choir director called a meeting. He stated these words. I have never forgotten them. "Praise the Lord! Yes, praise God! You know, God did wonderful things in this morning's service. But, I want you to know this: He didn't do them through you. He did them in spite of you. Now we have some work to do." The choir stood silently, fully accepting and agreeing with the stated truth.

Since that time, I have prayed sincerely that God would be able to minister through me rather than in spite of me. This desire forces me to prepare as thoroughly as possible. God has enough to overcome in the process without me simply not being prepared.

May God drive this truth deep into each of our hearts. He wants to minister through us, not in spite of our lack of preparation.

You can be your own best prop. In order to be that you will need to work. In order to present with excellence, you will need to practice. Don't shrink back, but press on to give God your best! Fill the jar to the brim!

Becoming a talented presenter requires an investment on the person's behalf. It is usually an investment of time, finances, sweat, and focus. A favorite quote of mine is, "Talent is wanting something bad enough to work for it." Talent is not simply a gift from God. Talent is what you develop with the potential God has given to you.

In our society, time is a precious commodity. Most children's ministers don't know where to locate an additional moment to learn new skills or polish the old ones. Here's what works for me.

I conscientiously take 20 minutes, either in the morning before breakfast or late at night before I go to bed, and invest that time in learning a new skill. If I only do this three times a week, that time still adds up to an hour. In a month, it adds up to four to five hours. In a year, that's fifty-two hours! In a year's time, I may become quite knowledgeable and proficient at a skill that I had no understanding of just a year ago! Fifty-two hours is a substantial amount of time. (Fact is, that's how I made time to write this book!)

Dr. Gordon Anderson, President of North Central University said this, "God doesn't want you to be a humble failure. He doesn't receive any glory from that! He wants you to be a humble success!"

Like the servants in Cana, it's time to fill up our "skill jars" to the brim, and let Jesus take it from there. He will do miracles if we will first do our part.

Ministry Applications:

#1. What time of day can you "whittle" away 15 minutes to learn a new skill? If you do this four times a week, that's one hour; in three months, that's thirteen hours; in a year, that's fifty-two hours!

_____

_____

_____

_____

_____

#2. Do you begin your lesson preparation far enough in advance to allow yourself time to polish your presentation techniques before the service time arrives? What time deadlines do you need to impose upon yourself in order to have enough time to prepare?

_____

_____

_____

_____

_____

#3. What can you do to be better prepared? Don't make excuses, but formulate a time plan to help you accomplish better preparation.

_____

_____

_____

_____

_____

Chapter Ten

The Outward Appearance

"Man looks on the outward appearance,
but the Lord looks on the heart".
1 Samuel 16:7 (NKJV)

There are two very important principles to consider that are listed in this scripture. The first one I want us to consider is the fact that, "God looks on the heart." As we develop ministries for children, we need to first of all make sure that our hearts are right. God looks on our heart. He knows our motives. That fact prompts these questions.

Are we involved in ministry to be recognized by others, or to be a servant? Are we seeking positions so we may be seen as people of power and authority? Some folks take joy in telling others what to do. That's why they work in the children's department. Children are easily intimidated and those leaders receive some type of warped emotional satisfaction knowing that they've verbally manipulated those kids into submission. Other specific leaders are working with children because they feel guilty of neglecting or hurting their children at some other time. Thus, they feel obligated now. If they work with children now, it will help their feeling of inadequacy in other areas. God sees our motives. He looks on the heart. He knows when we are lacking in pure motives.

On the other hand, some children's ministers choose to work in ministry out of an honest desire to bring a positive Christ-centered example to all ages. Many recognize the damaging effect of a selfish, non-God-centered society on children, and they desire to share Christ's love with these young ones so they can grow up with an understanding of His love. Various workers share that they want to help children avoid the spiritual pitfalls they fell into when they were youngsters.

A friend of mine grew up in an abusive home. Let's call her Rhoda. Her mother was emotionally manipulative. Her father was verbally and physically abusive. While in college, Rhoda answered the call to become involved with our clown ministry team. At first, I didn't know if she could portray a quality clown. Specifically, we visited children's hospitals, nursing homes and children's church services, and it didn't appear that Rhoda would be able to portray a loving persona. She offended others on the team and also was offended easily. Yet, she knew the pain with which some children lived. She wanted to make a difference in their lives, even if it was only for a few moments sharing a kind word, or playing on the floor with them.

Amazingly, as she continued to pray and develop her skills, I believe that God continued to develop her heart capacity. It wasn't long, and she became a favorite of audiences. She empathized with children in their weaknesses. God used the ministry of clowning to change her life. She found an avenue in which to express her heart.

God looks on our hearts. What are our motives? How does our heart beat for children? Once a person's heart is in line with God's heart, the expression comes naturally. We need to examine our hearts as we approach ministry and have our desires line up with God's desires.

Secondly, we need to recognize the fact that "man looks on the outward appearance." As people look on your ministry, what do they see? They don't immediately look in and see your heart. They see the outer shell. They don't have a deep enough relationship with you to know your heart, so all they may do is judge your ministry and motives by what they see on the outside. So, let me ask once again, what do they see?

A number of years ago I spoke with a ministry associate who dressed in the current style of the day. It was not a style that the parents of our church appreciated nor had their children wear. Simply, the style was neither neat or tidy. The church we served in was an upper middle-class Anglo mindset. I shared with my friend that though his heart was right, even if some of the children thought his contemporary attire was cutting edge and stylish, he was going to alienate himself from a number of the parents. They looked on the outward appearance! "Man looks on the outward appearance" (1 Samuel 16:7 NKJ V). Take that into consideration as you look at your own wardrobe and hairstyle. Do not use styles that raise questions in the minds of your onlookers.

People make assumptions by how you dress and present yourself. Some argue, "But people shouldn't do that!" Honestly, that may be correct, but that's not the issue. The fact is, people do make assumptions by how a person visually presents himself.

My friend Jeff was hired by a credit union to do some research concerning their various branches. In preparation for his unannounced visit he didn't shave for a week, didn't comb his hair, and donned worn old clothes. Once he arrived at the credit union he asked for help in obtaining a loan. He was held waiting for quite a period of time, but eventually made it through to an interview. He filled out the paperwork, but could tell that the creditor was uncomfortable with the thought of giving the loan. Jeff ended up leaving unsuccessful. He didn't obtain the loan.

About ten days later or so, Jeff showed up once again. This time he was clean-shaven and well dressed. He had even stopped for a haircut before his arrival at the place of business. Immediately, Jeff was addressed politely and processed through the application for a loan once again. Unbeknownst to the employees, this was the same man that had applied for a loan less than two weeks before. It only took a short period of time, and Jeff walked out of the credit union with loan papers in hand.

Jeff had accomplished the research his employers had desired and was able to help that business to make some positive changes in approach and policy. Were the employees at the credit union evil? No. They were simply influenced by the outward appearance. Scripture was clearly demonstrated. "Man looks on the outward appearance, but the Lord looks on the heart," 1 Samuel 16:7 (NKJV).

Another thing to consider: ask yourself if your ministry to children is viewed as struggling from the outside. Often children's ministers, when given an opportunity to address the congregation, stand up and wail about their lack of workers. They cry about the dismal ratio of helpers to kids in the preschool classroom. They whine about the one child who had behavior problems, rather than be complimentary about the fifty who were well behaved.

Consider what kind of picture that paints for those who are only viewing children's ministry from the outside. Why would they want to become involved in that type of "so-called-ministry?" It sounds like a nerve-wracking project!

I've found that people don't want to "get on board the sinking ship." They want to "jump on the band wagon!" So, look at what you are presenting to your people. What do they see from the outside? Is it a sinking ship breaking apart at the seams, or is it a bandwagon full of exciting and fun-loving music-makers?

People want to be involved in quality productions. They don't want to be involved with something that's failing. People are more likely to choose to be involved in a high caliber production than to commit to resuscitating a dying program. People don't like being around something that's dying. That's uncomfortable. They want to be involved with a ministry that's living and vibrant!

My friend, Jim Wideman, states, "If the appearance of evil can get you into trouble, then why can't the appearance of excellence help you?" Start giving the appearance of excellence to everything you do in children's ministries. Consider how you may give a heightened appearance of quality to everything you do. People will start believing that you have a quality ministry based upon the quality of your outward appearance.

Breathe exuberance into your promotions. Make it look like you are having a good time! Make people feel like they are missing out on something that is life-fulfilling, visionary, and eternally impacting if they are not currently involved. All those things are true anyway, aren't they? Promote on the positive side, not from the negative view.

You may already have a quality ministry, but a poor representation of it on the outside. Consequently, people will conclude that your ministry is weak based upon what they've seen.

Most parents only see the children's ministry in action during pre-service "check-in" and post-service "pick-up." In most churches, pre-service is the time when teachers are scurrying to set up crafts, finding supplies, communicating with their helpers about service plans, registering children, and listening to parental instruction about individual children. Children are crying, helpers are arriving late, and the lead teacher's frustration level is already mounting. It's chaotic.

When the service is done, parents are impatiently waiting at the door, Johnny spilled his kool-aid on his pants, and the craft papers are mixed up. Susy's mom states that Susy brought a beanie animal with her to class that has vanished. A mad search is conducted while others are trying to find their children's possessions. Sound familiar?

Since the pre-service and post-service times are when parents usually see the classroom in action, it's wise to focus on making these two time periods as efficient and pleasant as possible. Visiting parents will make judgments about your children's ministry based on these two time periods quickly. It doesn't seem fair to a children's worker, but that's the way it is. Those not involved in your ministry only look on the outward appearance. They have no other basis on which to judge it, so make sure you focus on the truly visible areas if you want to give them an accurate view of what your ministry is like.

Allow people to see that you are developing a quality program. Don't publicly focus on the negative aspects. Focus on those weaknesses in private. Strive for improvement with your leadership teams "behind closed doors." It would be wise to keep those areas you are working to improve out of the public eye.

What types of material do you send home with the children from your ministries? It's wise to look at the papers you're sending home. What does the quality of these materials tell parents and guardians? Do they help enhance your quality image, or do they cast a shadow of low-priority on the image of your ministry to children?

I remember a number of years ago when my son was four years old. Every Sunday, he came home with a coloring picture representing the Bible story he had listened to in Sunday School class. Every week he had scribbled a few multi-colored crayon lines on the picture. After a few months of this, my wife said to me, "Can't they find something more worthwhile to do than color every Sunday?! Can't there be a little more creativity than that?" Those were good questions. Understandably, we were making assumptions about my son's class based on what was sent home with him. We were not able to see what was happening on the inside of the class, but we did make judgements based on this "outward appearance." It's all we had on which to base our assumptions.

Consequently, since I want parents to have a positive view of ministry to their children I've determined to expose the parents to the quality experiences in which their children are participating. First of all, I always invite parents to stay and attend a children's service or activity with their child—especially first-time attenders. We have an "Open Door" policy with parents. They are always welcome. We want them to know that we don't have anything to hide and that we are there to team with them in making a positive difference in their children's lives.

Secondly, I've had "Open House" Sundays where specific families are invited to attend the children's services throughout the course of a month. For example: On the first Sunday of the month, families who have a last name beginning with letters "A" through "F" are invited to attend. On the second Sunday, families with a last name beginning with letters "G" through "N" are invited to attend; and so on.

In a smaller classroom setting, have a "Star of the Week" where the child brings a shoebox of articles that represent his different interests. Have the parents come to the class and tell an uplifting story about their child and compliment him on areas of growth and blessing in his life. Maybe they'd even bring a snack! By involving the parents and featuring the child, most parents will stay through the entirety of the class and receive a new perspective on what happens during your class session.

My goal is to expose entire families to the quality of ministry that we have for their children. Consequently, we also host "Family Specials" throughout the course of the year on regular week nights where families are invited to come for an evening of fun and ministry that all ages will enjoy. I'm trying to create opportunities for adults to see the inside heart and excitement of ministry to children.

While focusing on all of these specific visible items, remember to not just focus on what you are presenting outwardly. (That IS only the "wrapping," isn't it?) Strive to develop quality ministry. When you focus on quality, you will never need to worry about quantity. When people begin to see that you do effective ministry, workers will come. When you are meeting the needs of children in Jesus' name, more children will come. When your puppetry technique and ministry becomes absorbing to an audience, folks will come asking if they may be involved with your team. When people see that God is making a difference in you, and through you, they will want to be around you. The vision becomes contagious.

The quality draws the crowds. Never be concerned about trying to attract a quantity of people. Quantity is not the goal. Quality is the goal. If you will offer quality, the quantity will take care of itself.

Farmers know that the soil is the crucial element in planting and harvesting. A person cannot grow a thriving wheat field on a sand beach. The quality of the soil is a crucial element in the harvest.

Suffice it to say, have quality on the inside of your ministry, and also portray it on the outside, and God will take care of the growth.

MINISTRY APPLICATIONS:

#1. Since parents usually only look on the outside of your children's ministries, consider how you may give them a quality image of what is happening with their children. Rate the quality of the appearance of these items that parents may be looking at: ("0" for poor, "5" for excellent)

ITEM

Take home papers

0   1   2   3   4   5

Newsletters and mailers

0   1   2   3   4   5

Announcement fliers

0   1   2   3   4   5

Crafts

0   1   2   3   4   5

Children's room decorations

0   1   2   3   4   5

Appearance of registration area

0   1   2   3   4   5

Visitor information packet

0   1   2   3   4   5

Preservice "check-in" format

0   1   2   3   4   5

Post-service "pick-up" time

0   1   2   3   4   5

Other

0   1   2   3   4   5

#2. What can be done to improve each of these areas? You may have a number that has rated in the poor category. If so, focus on the simplest one first. After improving that area, move on to the next. Work on one area at a time. By doing this, you will gain positive momentum.

_____

_____

_____

_____

_____

_____

#3. If you are in leadership; to maintain and improve quality of ministry, you must communicate positively, clearly and consistently with those you supervise in children's ministry. Rate yourself on these areas: ("0" for poor, "5" for excellent)

Consistent advance communication

0   1   2   3   4   5

Clear written communication & forms

0   1   2   3   4   5

Clear communication of vision

0   1   2   3   4   5

Regular appreciation shared

0   1   2   3   4   5

Teacher training made available

0   1   2   3   4   5

#4. If you are willing to be daring, you may want to have some of your key children's ministry team evaluate each of these areas for you. If you do this, make sure that you are prepared to receive honest critique without being personally offended. Your worker's perspectives may be quite different than your own.

_____

_____

_____

_____

#5. What can you do to improve each of these areas? You may want to list each of these areas quarterly on your annual calendar so you will be reminded to give focus to each of these on a regular basis.

_____

_____

_____

_____

#6. When speaking to others (specifically pastoral leadership), develop the good habit of speaking of the great things that God is doing in your ministry. Give them something to praise God for! Don't focus on the negatives. If you need to discuss areas that need improvement, schedule a specific meeting with your direct supervisor. Don't "ambush" him while in the hallway between services!

_____

_____

_____

_____

Chapter Eleven

Children In Worship: Worship In Children

I used to think that I needed to teach children how to worship. I would teach them how to lift their hands; how to behave appropriately during a worship service; how to bow their heads in prayer. I would affect the "blank slate" of their lives with teaching from the Word of God and from my prior experience. That's what I thought.

Well, I was wrong. As stated earlier, Psalm 8:2 (NIV) shares, "From the mouths of children and infants you have ordained praise because of your enemies, to silence the foe and the avenger." Jesus quotes that verse to the chief priests and the teachers of the law as the children shouted Christ's praises in the temple area (Matthew 21:16). Our Lord didn't say, "It's amazing that someone taught these kids to praise God! Just listen to them!" No, he stated that God Himself has ordained praise from the mouths of even the very youngest.

Still today, God is calling forth praise even from young ones! We simply need to push back the barriers and open the gates that hold children back from praising God. We need to be like the mothers who brought the children to Jesus, not like the disciples who shooed them away. We need to be the ones who lead the procession of children to "enter His gates with thanksgiving and his courts with praise" (Psalm 100:4 NIV).

We don't need to teach them to praise. Praise is an innate desire. It's what we were created to do! Think of it this way. I don't need to teach my dog to bark. He was made to bark! When it comes to leading children in worship, or anyone for that matter, we simply need to help eliminate the barriers that keep them from joining in heartfelt worship!

Song Selection

We should worship with all of our heart, soul, mind and strength (Mark 12:30) so that children may imitate us and follow us into a vibrant worship atmosphere. This will not happen by having a steady stream of "Father Abraham" action choruses though. We need to lead children in meaningful declaration through song!

The importance of song selection for worship times has been etched deeply in my heart. A number of years ago, Dave, one of my bus captains, returned from taking the children home on the church bus after a Saturday morning outreach. Dave pulled me aside and told me this story:

> Today on the bus, we were singing songs, as we often do, and one of the other workers asked the

kids what they'd like to sing. Josh, a boy about nine-years-old, raised his hand and asked that we sing his favorite song, "Only Jesus." The workers looked at each other perplexed. They had never heard the song. They asked Josh if he would sing it for them anyway. Joshua's voice rose sweetly: "Only Jesus...has the power...of salvation...in His blood. Only Jesus...has the power...of salvation...in His blood." The workers sat, with tears in their eyes. Broken voiced, Dave asked, "Josh, where did you learn that?" Josh replied, 'Here at bus ministry two years ago.'"

You see, Dave and the others on the bus hadn't been serving in bus ministry at that time. They had never learned the song. But that young boy had, and for the past two years he had been walking through his non-Christian home proclaiming through song, "Only Jesus...has the power...of salvation...in his blood." It was his favorite song. How thankful I was that I had taught a song with doctrinal life-changing substance two years previously!

These are the truths that need to be etched into children's lives. Songs that truly carry hope; songs that carry the gospel; songs that bring children into the presence of God through heartfelt worship. It's time to leave behind "Climb Up Sunshine Mountain," and start teaching, "Only Jesus...has the power...of salvation...in His blood."

Eliminating Barriers

If children are not entering into a life-giving worship experience, it generally is because the leaders have not yet caught the vision for it. Children only go as far as we will lead. They are followers. We need to move in front of them and eliminate the barriers that keep them from worshiping. We need to pull out that "Holy Spirit-machete" and clear a trail so they may approach the presence of God!

Here are a number of barriers with which the children in my church struggle:

#1. The fear of doing it wrong: Children want to be successful. An example comes to mind: Some are afraid to lift their hands, because they might do it wrong and look bad in front of their friends, or think they may be publicly corrected. Give clear instructions during worship times, and this barrier will be removed.

#2. The fear of peer pressure: If twenty boys are sitting together, usually one of two things happen. Either all of them stand up, or none of them do. Either all of them sing, or none of them do. Either none of them lift their hands in worship, or all of them do. Usually "none" seems to be the normal response. I simply eliminate peer pressure by requiring the appropriate response by all present. That's right. I REQUIRE appropriate response.

Example: I tell all of the children to lift their hands during a final chorus. This way, those who desired to lift their hands may lift their hands without feeling pressured by their friends' non-participation. Their friends are participating. They're required to. At the same time those who don't want to lift their hands may discover that it's part of a fulfilling worship experience. It may be that they've never done it before.

Sometimes my children at home don't want to try a new dish at the supper table. What do I do? I require them to taste it. I make them give it a try.

Some don't feel that requiring response is the best way to remove this barrier. I do. As children's ministry leaders we are not being uncaring or mean by asking a child to lift his hands in the air to worship God for thirty seconds out of a week!

Another way to remove this barrier is to actually turn it around and use peer pressure positively. I do this by having a worship team of children helping lead the other children in worship. When my worship team of children are pouring their hearts out to God, the other children see them and follow their lead. I'm setting a group of their peers up as examples to them. I'm using peer pressure positively. We are showing the children in the chairs that worship is not only something that adults do, it's also something that children their age participate in.

#3. Apathy: We need to help children understand that God is worthy of praise, even when we don't feel like worshiping Him! We need to be Bible-based, thankful, faith-motivated people. We need to help children learn to choose to worship God, even when their fickle emotions are telling them not to. Yes, God wants heartfelt worship. But, for many people, heartfelt worship will never be achieved until they first of all make it an act of the will and simply choose to do it because it's the right thing to do! Scripture continually exhorts us to praise God. It doesn't say, "Praise God when you feel like it."

Psalm 22:3 (KJV) states that God inhabits the praises of His people. If we truly desire God's presence to be manifested in our services, we will expect children to join in worship. This is for their own good! Children will not experience the presence of God unless they begin to worship Him!

Often, when leading children in worship, I pause and ask these young saints, "How many of you really didn't feel like worshiping God when you came in here today, but then you started to worship God anyway, and now you can sense that God is really here in this place, and He's changing how you've felt?" Often, numerous children will respond affirmatively.

I'm simply helping them internalize and apply the truth, "If you will do what is right, the feelings will follow." We don't wait for our feelings to tell us what to do. We do what is right first, and then our feelings will eventually get in line with it. This is a key application of faith. We live by our convictions and the truth of God's Word, not by our wavering emotions.

So, don't apologize for asking all the children to respond during a time of worship. Do it lovingly and clearly. This is for their own spiritual growth.

#4. Volume: Many people are self-conscious. Most don't believe they have pleasant singing voices. They are afraid that others will hear them. Older elementary-aged boys don't want others to hear their voices break and squeak!

I've found that the quieter the accompaniment is, the quieter everyone sings. The louder it is, the louder people sing. Within reason, people will match their vocal volume with the instrumental music. Turning up your volume will allow the most monotone singer to join in without fear.

#5. Terminology: Examine the words that you are using. Are they a barrier or an aid? Are your words easily understandable and applicable? Do the children understand what it means when you say that Jesus is our "atoning sacrifice?" If they don't, you may not want to sing the song that says that. Otherwise, make sure to take the time and clearly explain what this means.

I stood in front of a large church's children's choir. I asked them, "What does the word 'hallelujah' mean?" I waited. Out of one hundred and forty children, three raised their hands to give me the answer. Not one of them was right.

Often, we have used our Christian terminology to such an extent that we forget that children may not understand what we are saying. They may not understand what they are saying as they repeat it back to us! We think that they will somehow begin to understand our Christian jargon if they just say it enough times. This is errant thinking.

Jesus quoted Isaiah in Matthew 15:8,9 (NIV) "These people honor me with their lips, but their hearts are far from me. They worship me in vain; their teachings are but rules taught by men."

Our objective must be to lead children to worship in spirit and in truth (John 4:24). They need to have an understanding of what they are saying if they are going to worship in truth. 1 Corinthians 14:15 (NKJV) states that we sing in the spirit, and we also sing with the understanding. Impart understanding! Don't assume that children understand the words of the songs, or the reasons that we demonstrate worship the way we do. Break open scripture for them. Help them see the validity of what they are doing. This will make the worship time relevant to their lives and will give purpose and meaning to their worship expression today and in the years to come.

Once again, we don't have to teach children to praise. God is calling forth praise, even from the very youngest! We simply need to push back the barriers that hold children back from praising God. We need to be the ones who lead the procession of children to "enter His gates with thanksgiving and His courts with praise" (Psalm 100:4 NIV).

MINISTRY APPLICATION:

#1. Are there barriers that are keeping your children from entering into worship? What are they?

_____

_____

_____

_____

#2. Are there barriers that are keeping you and other leadership from entering into Biblical patterns of worship? Identify them and purpose to make a personal change.

_____

_____

_____

_____

#3. Study Biblical patterns of worship. At the beginning of each of your services, teach a four to five minute segment on worship then lead the children in responding to the Lord using the Biblical mode.

_____

_____

_____

_____

MINISTRY APPLICATIONS

Endnotes

A s we come to the close of this book, I'd like to share three specific thoughts about ministry to children.

First of all, my personal experience testifies to the fact that ministering to children will not only change the children's lives, but the worker's as well. As we pray, practice, ponder, and present, God will work in us and through us. He will mold us as we offer ourselves to Him as willing vessels. 2 Corinthians 4:7 states, "We have this treasure in jars of clay..." (NIV). We are the jars being molded by the Maker. We are the jars that carry the treasure of God's grace to these young ones. One cannot be full of the message of God's love without being changed by it.

We are like new wineskins filled with new living vibrant wine. That "new wine" is the message we carry to these young ones. A wineskin, once filled with new wine, stretches. The new wine affects that wineskin. We cannot carry the message of Christ without being affected by it. It's exciting to be changed by the Holy Spirit as we prepare for ministry and as we minister. Philippians 2:13 tells us that God's Spirit works in us both, "to will and to act according to his good purpose."

While preparing to minister we immerse ourselves in the study of the Word and prayer. That changes us. "The word of God is quick and powerful," (Hebrews 4:12 KJV). Through a continued life of studying scripture and of prayer, a children's worker is changed! I am a better person because of my involvement in ministry to children.

Romans 12:2 states, "Be ye transformed by the renewing of your mind" (KJV). I need to continue to be transformed. It's crucial that each of us become the leaders that God desires for us to be. He needs people like me. He needs people like you! "Dear Holy Spirit, change us we cry! Fill us with the treasure of your love so that it may be poured out to those you've entrusted to us!"

Secondly, it's time to minister to children. There's no excuse for delay. This facet of the body of Christ is essential. The local church, and the Church Universal, cannot be healthy without all of it's body parts being strong. 1 Corinthians 12:14 (NKJV) teaches, "...the body is not one member, but many." Romans 12:4,5 (NIV) shares, "Just as each of us has one body with many members, and these members do not all have the same function, so in Christ we who are many form one body, and each member belongs to all the others." Each person, even the youngest, is an important part of Christ's body of believers. We dare not ignore this part of the body. It's crucial. If they suffer, the entire body will suffer. If they thrive, it will help the rest of the body to increase.

It's time to focus upon this incredible harvest field. "The fields are white unto harvest..." Jesus said, "...but the laborers are few" (Mark 4:35 KJV).

A farmer knows that once the field is white, his labor in that field must become the highest priority. If he delays, some of the harvest may be lost. My father-in-law is a farmer in South Dakota. He looks for the moment that the crops are ready. Once the fields are ripe he works around the clock to bring in that harvest. Nothing is of higher priority. The harvest must be brought in.

Jesus also stated, "To enter the kingdom of God you must become as a child" (Matthew 18:3 NIV). Consider the implications of that statement in relationship to the harvest analogy. Logically, if we must become like children to enter God's kingdom, we can deduce that children must somehow be closer to entering the kingdom than adults are. Otherwise, Jesus would have said, "To enter the kingdom of God you must become like an adult." But, He didn't say that. He said, "Become as a child." It makes it easier.

Statistics from numerous organizations (including the Billy Graham Association and Child Evangelism Fellowship) show clearly that well over three quarters of the people who are believers today accepted Christ as children. Children are more open to the gospel than adults are as a whole. That's why Jesus said that a person needs to become as a child to enter the kingdom.

The field of children is ripe. When a person is young, it's truly "harvest time!" It's time to reach, teach and disciple them. It's time to get into the fields. We must not delay!

The harvest is serious business. It does not make sense for the farmer to procrastinate, and then try to salvage fruit that is rotting on the vine. He needs to pick the fruit when it's at optimum stage. As we work with children, that is what we are doing in the spiritual arena. The fields are white when people are young. Let's go bring them in!

Some people gather roses
along the road of life.
Others gather money to cease
from earthly strife.
But, I will gather children
from among the thorns of sin.
I'd rather choose a golden curl,
or a freckled toothless grin.
For money will not enter that
land of endless day.
And flowers that you gather
will wilt along the way.
But, oh, the laughing children,
when I cross the sunset sea,
When the gates of heaven swing open wide,
I can take them in with me!

-Author Unknown

"Let us not become weary in doing good, for at the proper time we will reap a harvest if we do not give up" (Galatians 6:9 NIV).

Lastly, you and I must accept the challenge to not only teach children, but truly become people that others may follow. Be a person of prayer. Be a true worshiper. Be a student of God's Word and of the culture and needs of children. Be humble and teachable.

May God work through you as you seek His heart and vision for the children He's entrusted to you. May God lead, guide and empower you in the days ahead!

Serving His Children,

Rev. Randy Christensen

MINISTRY APPLICATIONS:

#1. Mark 16:15 commands us to "Go into all the world and preach the good news" (NIV). Think and pray for discernment on how you may enter into the world of the child in order to preach the good news to him.

_____

_____

_____

_____

#2. Jesus calls us to be "fishers of men" (Matthew 4:19). A person knows he cannot catch any fish if he's not casting out the net into the water. What are you doing to get out where the "fish" are? Where may you find a "school of fish" where you may throw some spiritual bait? (i.e., parks, after school programs, backyards, parades, community centers, holiday events, etc.)

_____

_____

_____

_____

#3. Evaluate where the most popular children's events and activities take place in your area. Write down six reasons why each activity is popular with children. Ask "Why do children want to go back?" Are you able to add any of these elements into your children's pro-gramming, even in small ways?

_____

_____

_____

MINISTRY APPLICATIONS

_____

_____

_____

#4. In the parable of the Great Banquet, the servants were told by the Master to go into the highways and byways and compel people to come in. What can you do to make children feel compelled to come and hear the gospel? (i.e., exciting visuals, rewards, special guests, crafts, prayer, etc.)

_____

_____

_____

_____

About the Author

Rev. Randy Christensen began working with children as a college student in 1980. Since then, Randy has ministered to children, families, and children's workers around the world. He's an accomplished clown, variety arts performer, worship leader, composer, and author.

Randy resides in Rockford, Illinois with his wife, Karen, and their three children, Ben, Brooke & Shane.

Resources By Randy

Randy has written and produced numerous booklets, worship leading tapes, CD's, and videos to help those in children's ministry and clown ministry. Randy hosts workshops and training opportunities for children's workers and clown ministers.

BOOKS

Clowning For Christ

Clown Skits . . . For Christ

Developing Clown Ministry Programs

Solo Clown Ministry

Clown Tradition

Comic Ministry Routines

Comic Ministry Routines 2

Clown Fun For Everyone

Easy Gospel Cartoons

Cartoon Lessons

Costumes and Characters

Tithe Talks

Tithe Talks Two

Worship Insights

The Directors Desk

MUSIC

Hymns For the Ages
Creative Performance
Creative Performance 2
Creative Performance 3
Checkerboard Rap
The Highest of Praise
My Choice

VIDEOS

Lights, Camera, Clowning
Kid Relevant Kid's Church, Vol. 1
Kid Relevant Kid's Church, Vol. 2
The Water Baptism Video

. . . and more! @ www.RandysInfo.com

Author Contact Information

For information on Randy's availability for worker train-ing events or upcoming conferences, you may contact:

Randy Christensen
c/o Rockford First Assembly
5950 Spring Creek Road
Rockford, IL 61114
On the web: www.RandysInfo.com